D0913065

Wheel of Time

WHEEL OF
TIME

Harry Zarchy

Illustrated by René Martin

62

THOMAS Y. CROWELL COMPANY · NEW YORK

By the Author

WHEEL OF TIME

USING ELECTRONICS

BUILDING WITH ELECTRONICS

Manufactured in the United States of America
by the Vail-Ballou Press, Inc., Binghamton, New York

LIBRARY OF CONGRESS CATALOG CARD NO. 57-10282

Seventh Printing

For Bill and Sue,
David and Mark,
Andy and Amy,
and their wonderful parents

INTRODUCTION

EVERYTHING we do is regulated by calendars, clocks and watches. We think of events as having taken place at a particular time. They may be remembered as having occurred on a certain day; you may even recall the exact hour. Minutes, hours, days, weeks, months and years are names man has devised to indicate the passage of time. Calendars, clocks and watches are mechanisms invented by man to enable him to measure time.

What time is it? Will the train be on time? Is it time for lunch? Will you be late for school or work? How long will it take to do the job? When is your birthday? Will you take your vacation during the summer? Our daily references to time are so common that we take them for granted and attach no unusual significance to them. This is because of our ability to measure time.

INTRODUCTION

Nothing in our daily lives is exempt from our dependence upon time. Travel, communications, business, social affairs, governmental operations—all depend upon strict adherence to definite time standards.

In short, our earth and everything on it *runs on time!*

HARRY ZARCHY
FREEPORT, NEW YORK

CONTENTS

1

TIME AND MOTION

TIME is motion. This is a simple fact that can easily be explained.

Let us begin with the idea that *years* and *days,* our two basic time divisions, are based upon movements of the earth.

YEARS

The earth and all the other planets in our solar system are in constant motion. They revolve around the sun in fixed paths, called *orbits*. The time needed for a planet to make one complete revolution around the sun is called a *year*. The closer a planet is to the sun, the faster it travels; it also moves in a smaller orbit than those farther away. Consequently, the planets nearest the sun have the shortest years, while those farther away have years of correspondingly longer length.

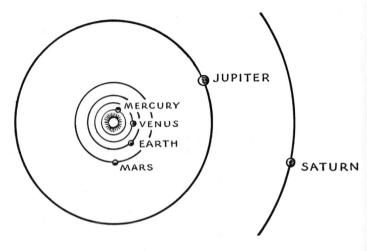

The earth makes a complete revolution in approximately 365¼ days. It might be interesting to compare our year with those of the other planets:

Planet	Length of Year (Earth time)
MERCURY	88 days
VENUS	225 days
EARTH	365.26 days
MARS	687 days
JUPITER	11.9 years
SATURN	29.5 years
URANUS	84 years
NEPTUNE	164.8 years
PLUTO	248.4 years

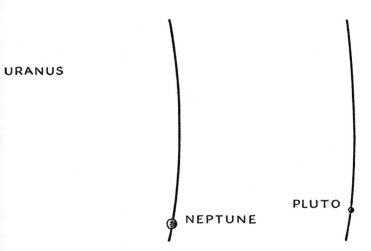

URANUS

PLUTO

NEPTUNE

Since the planets have years of different length, their
inhabitants (purely imaginary, of course) would each
have different concepts of a year. They would reckon
time according to the revolutions of their particular
planets. Continuing this little fantasy, let us imagine a
group of people born at the same time on different
planets. They would always be the same biological age,
for their bodies would grow and mature at the same rate.
However, their chronological ages would be a different
story, for time would be calculated differently on each
planet.

Let us glance at another table and see approximately
how old a one-year-old Earth baby would be considered
on each planet of the solar system:

3

Planet	*Age* (as reckoned on each planet)
MERCURY	4.13 years
VENUS	1.6 years
EARTH	1 year
MARS	.53 year
JUPITER	.083 year
SATURN	.034 year
URANUS	.012 year
NEPTUNE	.0061 year
PLUTO	.0040 year

Obviously, traveling in space presents its own peculiar problems, for we need a separate timekeeping system for each planet.

DAYS

Each planet not only revolves around the sun, but it also spins, or rotates, on its axis at the same time. The axis does not actually exist; it is an imaginary line which runs through the center of a planet, from pole to pole. The earth's axis extends from North Pole to South Pole and the earth spins around on it.

The time taken by a planet to make one complete turn on its axis is called a *day*. Since the planets rotate at different speeds, they have days of different length:

4

Planet	Length of Day (Earth time)
MERCURY	88 days
VENUS	225 days
EARTH	24 hours, or 1 day
MARS	24 hours, 40 minutes
JUPITER	9 hours, 55 minutes
SATURN	10 hours, 14 minutes
URANUS	10 hours, 8 minutes
NEPTUNE	15 hours, 40 minutes
PLUTO	Unknown

Light from the sun can strike only one side of the earth at any time. Because the earth rotates, most places have alternating periods of daylight (day), and darkness (night).

Let us suppose that the earth's axis is perpendicular to the plane of its orbit, the path in which it travels around the sun. If this were so, one half of the earth would always be illuminated by the sun, *from pole to pole*. As the earth rotated, every place between the North Pole and the South Pole would have 12 hours of daylight and 12 hours of night. Days and nights would be of equal length, every day of the year, every place on earth.

However, days and nights are not of equal length

5

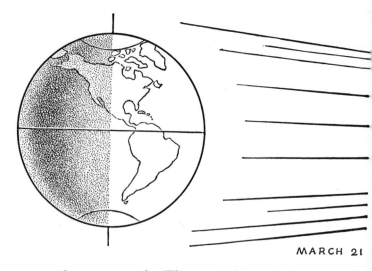

MARCH 21

every place on earth. The most important reason for this inequality is the fact that the earth's axis is *not* perpendicular but *inclined,* or slanted at an angle of 23½ degrees. If days are longer than nights in the Northern Hemisphere, then nights are longer than days in the Southern Hemisphere.

The next illustration shows the position of the earth as it appears on June 21. Notice that the sun's rays do not illuminate the earth evenly from pole to pole, as in the preceding diagram. Instead, the North Pole is tilted toward the sun. The Northern Hemisphere, which faces the sun, will have longer days than nights, because more of it is exposed to the sun's rays. The Southern Hemisphere will have short days and long nights.

6

Let us analyze the diagram and see exactly why this happens. The shaded areas represent night. At the equator, exactly one half of the earth has day, while the other half has night. Since the earth rotates once every 24 hours, every part of the equator will pass through equal periods of illumination and darkness; days and nights will be 12 hours long.

TROPIC OF CANCER

EQUATOR

TROPIC OF CAPRICORN

JUNE 21

As we move north from the equator, more and more of the Northern Hemisphere is exposed to the sun's rays. Slightly more than half of the Tropic of Cancer is in daylight. The length of day at that point would therefore be slightly more than half the earth's 24-hour rotational period, or about 13 hours. The farther north we go, the longer the days become, until the Arctic Circle is reached. From here to the North Pole there is no night at all, for the whole area lies within the daylight zone. At this time, it is summer in the Northern Hemisphere.

Move south from the equator and conditions are reversed. The Southern Hemisphere which faces away from the sun and lies mostly in darkness is having winter. As we approach the South Pole, the nights grow longer and the days become shorter. The earth south of the Antarctic Circle remains in 24-hour darkness during the winter.

Days are longest during the summer and gradually become shorter through the autumn. They are shortest during winter, and then slowly lengthen during spring, until they finally reach their summer span again. This change takes place all over the earth, except at the equator.

Let us review some of the facts we have learned, so that we may organize our thoughts:

8

1. The earth rotates on its axis; this gives us day and night.

2. The earth's axis is tilted; as a result, most of the Northern Hemisphere or most of the Southern Hemisphere is facing the sun.

3. The hemisphere facing the sun receives more light over a greater area. Days will be longer than nights.

4. The hemisphere facing away from the sun receives less light. Days will be shorter than nights.

What do you suppose would be the result if the earth did not revolve around the sun but remained in one position? Our illustration shows the answer. Since there would be no change in their relative positions, the amount of light received by each hemisphere would not

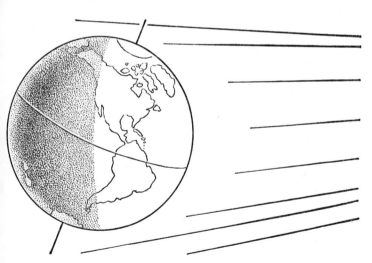

change. Days and nights would remain the same length, *and would never vary*. Accordingly, the North Pole would have eternal daylight and the South Pole would forever remain in darkness. If the earth were on the other side of the sun, the North Pole would be doomed to constant night and the South Pole would be exposed to unchanging sun.

The movement of the earth around the sun decidedly has something to do with the changes in the length of our days and nights.

The next picture shows the earth in its journey around the sun. No matter where the earth may be in its orbit, its axis always points in the same direction—toward the North Star. Astronomers refer to this as *parallelism*. The earth's axis at any given time is parallel to any other position it may have in the orbit.

Now let us see how both the revolution of the earth and its parallelism affect the length of day and night. Here we show four positions of the earth during the year. We are familiar with the situation on June 21, for at that time the Northern Hemisphere is fully tilted toward the sun. It receives its maximum amount of light; this is the longest day of the year for us in the Northern Hemisphere. On the same day, the Southern Hemisphere, which faces away from the sun, receives its minimum amount of light; this is its shortest day.

10

Let us follow the progress of the earth in its orbit. As it moves, the position of its axis in relation to the sun changes, and the Northern Hemisphere receives a little less sunlight. The change takes place very gradually, day by day. By the time earth reaches its position of approximately September 23, the Northern Hemisphere no longer receives the greater portion of sunlight. Both hemispheres receive equal amounts of light; days and nights will be of approximately equal length every place on earth.

When the earth reaches its position of December 21, it will be the reverse of its June 21 position. Because the earth's axis is parallel to itself (points in the same direction) on both of these days, the Southern Hemisphere will then be fully inclined toward the sun, and it will have its longest day. The Northern Hemisphere, facing away from the sun, has its shortest day. As the earth continues in its path around the sun, days will gradually change in length until March 21, when both hemispheres will again share equally in the amount of sunlight received. Once more, days and nights will be equal all over the earth.

The two days when day and night are equal in length are known as *equinoxes*—"equal night." September 23 is known as the *fall equinox,* and March 21 is the *spring equinox.*

It is impossible to discuss the reasons for unequal days and nights without touching upon the seasons. The same factors that determine the duration of days and nights are responsible for seasonal changes as well. Briefly, they are:

1. The earth's axis is inclined.
2. It is parallel to itself throughout its orbit.
3. The earth revolves about the sun in a fixed orbit.

We now know that as the earth makes its annual journey around the sun the Northern and Southern Hemispheres alternately receive greater portions of sunlight. Because the earth's orbit is always the same, and its revolution always takes the same length of time, we experience a *regular* change of seasons. We generally

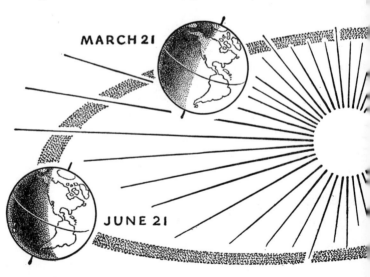

regard June 21 as the beginning of summer in the Northern Hemisphere and September 23 as the first day of autumn. December 21 generally ushers in our winter and March 21 inaugurates spring.

A full discussion of the seasons, however, would take us far afield from our present study. It would have to include numerous important facts which are not relevant here.

Moreover, the purpose of this chapter is to show that *time is motion,* and that all our ideas about time—years, seasons and days—are all derived from the movements of heavenly bodies. It is quite obvious that if the earth and the other planets in the solar system were stationary, we would have no concept of time.

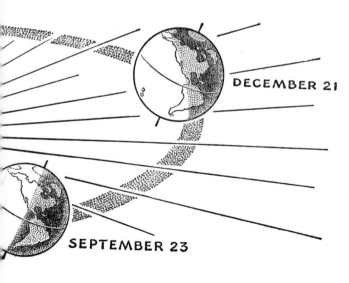

2

YEARS AND MONTHS

THE calendar provides us with a system for reckoning time, measuring time intervals, and establishing dates. It is a device to help us fix the relations between the days of the year and the positions of the earth in its revolution around the sun.

The calendar makes it possible for us to locate specific dates in time. If we speak of something as having taken place on March 21, we think not only of a certain day and month but also of a specific season. Since the seasons are determined by the relative positions of the earth in its orbit, then March 21 must occur when the earth is in the same position each year.

This happens because the number of days in our calendar matches the number of days in the year. Our year has been computed as having 365 days, 5 hours, 48 minutes, and 46 seconds. This is known as the *tropical*, or *solar*, year. It is roughly designated as having

14

365¼ days. If our calendar had only 365 days, it would be faster than the solar year by ¼ of a day each year. At the end of 4 years it would be 1 full day ahead. As time went on, this difference would increase, until, at the end of 120 years, our calendar would be advanced by 1 whole month. The first day of spring would no longer fall on March 21 but on February 19. All of our seasons would be out of line and would occur earlier and earlier each year. Eventually we would have winter weather in July and August and summer heat waves in December and January!

The problem of the extra quarter-day each year has been solved very neatly by making use of leap years. Every fourth year we add an extra day to the month of February and bring ourselves up to date.

The development of the calendar is a fascinating story that has its origins in the dim, prehistoric past. Let us go back to the days of primitive man and imagine what might have taken place.

Primitive man's first clock was the sun. Day after day it rose above the eastern horizon and created light. It moved slowly across the sky and then sank out of sight in the west, plunging the world into darkness. The regular, unfailing appearance and disappearance of the sun impressed itself upon the mind of man. Day and night—the periods of light and darkness—were the

15

first definite time intervals with which he became familiar.

During the day, prehistoric man hunted, fished, worked, traveled, and conducted his daily affairs. He kept watch for his enemies and took security precautions at the first sign of danger from man or beast. All this was possible because the sun gave him light and warmth.

Night was a time of insecurity and terror. The friendly sun was gone, and in its place was the dreaded darkness. People sought shelter wherever they could, often using natural caves. Fires provided light and heat. No one ventured beyond the firelight's protection, for danger lurked everywhere. There were huge, predatory animals and worse—terrible spirits, creatures of man's imagination.

Since daytime was the period of man's activity, it was quite logical for him to begin to reckon time by referring to "suns." He may have done this by gathering together a number of pebbles, one for each "sun," or by cutting notches in a stick, or by making drawings of the sun on a stone with a piece of charcoal.

Our early ancestors were also very much aware of the other heavenly bodies. They could see the moon making its nightly journey across the sky. They must have wondered about many things. Why did the moon change

16

its appearance every night? Why did it disappear, and where did it go?

Then came a time when people evolved a primitive method of counting. They tallied the number of suns between full moons and found that this number, about 29 suns, always remained the same. They learned to anticipate the advent of the full moon, then to think of longer time intervals, or "moons." Instead of referring to 29 suns, they simply indicated one "moon."

The stars, too, fascinated prehistoric man. Why were some brighter than others? Why were certain stars grouped together, revolving across the sky in permanent patterns? The stars seemed to be part of the vast procession in the heavens, where everything moved in an orderly manner. As the days wore on, certain groups of stars disappeared over the horizon and others appeared

17

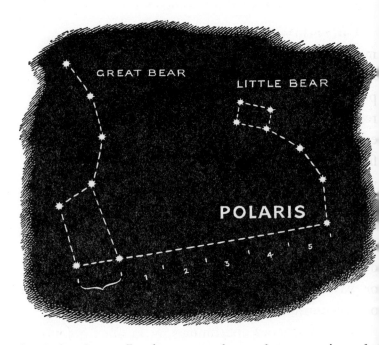

in their places. In time, men learned to associate the
appearance of particular star groups with the coming of
each season. They may even have given them names,
so that they could be identified more easily. They also
discovered that one constellation remained in the same
place in the heavens. In this constellation was Polaris,
the North Star.

Archaeologists have found recognizable sky charts
drawn on the walls of ancient caves, proving that early
man was aware of the constellations. Who knows to
what extent this knowledge was utilized?

18

Early man was a hunter. In order to survive, he had to move from place to place in search of food—game, fruits, berries, nuts, roots and grain. A tribe would probably find an area in which food was plentiful and remain as long as the supply held out. This type of existence lasted for many thousands of years. Man had no fixed home.

Eventually, he ceased to be a wandering hunter and settled in a permanent place. His mode of living changed because he learned to grow crops. It is interesting to speculate about how this happened. Did someone accidentally discover that new plants sprouted from seeds, or was this new knowledge the result of long, careful observation?

With these crude beginnings as farmers, the tribes remained in the vicinity of their crops in order to protect them from other tribes and wild animals. The wanderers began to build permanent homes of enduring materials and settled down.

But men still depended upon hunting for their basic food supply. It was a long time before they acquired and domesticated animals for this purpose. As flocks and herds increased in size, the animals' offspring became familiar with the sight and smell of man. Eventually, domesticated animals furnished men with all the meat they needed; hunting was no longer necessary.

Man, the hunter, had little need for an accurate calendar. Man, the farmer, was forced to develop one. He had to anticipate the seasons and, for the first time, plan ahead. He discovered that his crops had to be sown at a certain time, so that they would be ready for harvesting before winter. His new way of life demanded a knowledge of the seasons and an accurate way of predicting their arrival.

No one knows when the first calendar was developed, but it seems fairly certain that it was based upon "moons," or lunar months. The ancient hunters knew about moons, and it is possible that their tribal wise men or witch doctors had worked out rough lunar calendars. In this they were no doubt guided by various phenomena of nature, such as the falling of leaves, the budding of trees and flowers, the hibernation of animals, migrations of birds and other seasonal events.

When man gave up his old nomadic ways, these tribal wise men were elevated to positions of great importance. They studied the heavens vigilantly and gradually accumulated enough knowledge of astronomy to be able to forecast seasonal changes fairly accurately. They alone had the necessary knowledge, and they maintained their importance by establishing rituals of sorcery and magic. This knowledge was restricted to a small, carefully selected group. Thus, a new, powerful class arose

—a priesthood. In return for their special services, the priests were supported by their fellow villagers and accorded great respect.

In time, civilizations based on grazing, trade and crop cultivation developed in different parts of the world. One of the most ancient was found in southwestern Asia, in the valleys of the Tigris and Euphrates Rivers. The Greeks called this land Mesopotamia, which means, "land between two rivers." This is the region in which many of the events mentioned in the Old Testament are said to have taken place. Here the cultures of the Sumerians, the Assyrians and the Chaldeans flourished and faded. Babylon was situated here, with its Tower of Babel and its Hanging Gardens, which were considered one of the Seven Wonders of the Ancient World.

Babylon represented a high degree of civilization. Its houses were well constructed of sun-dried brick. The walls of the temples and the king's palace were decorated with murals executed in brilliant ceramic tile. Dominating the entire city was a square pyramid, about 600 feet high, called a *ziggurat*. It was built on several levels, each painted a different color and each sacred to a particular god. The different levels were reached by a series of ramps which spiraled upward around the outside of the structure. At the top was a shrine dedicated to Marduk, the chief god of the city of Babylon.

21

The ziggurat was a holy place, and it was probably used as an astronomical observatory by the Babylonian priests. Since the ancient Babylonian-Chaldeans worshipped the sun, the moon and the stars, astronomy played a very important part in their lives. The priests studied the heavens constantly and made shrewd deductions from their observations. In time they became firmly established as the most powerful group in the land. Without the use of the telescope or other modern astronomical instruments, they scanned the skies and learned about the progress of the heavenly bodies. The amount of accurate information they amassed is truly astonishing.

They discovered five of our planets, and worshipped them as gods. Mars was *Nergal*, Venus was *Ishtar*, Jupiter was *Marduk*, Saturn was *Ninib*, and Mercury was *Nibo*. They also worshiped the moon as *Nannar*, or *Sin*, the sun was the god *Shamash*.

The priest-astronomers also developed a lunar calendar. They observed that it took about 30 days for the moon to go through its phases, from full moon to full moon; this became their month. The year consisted of 12 months, each having 30 days. If they had used 13 months, their calendar would have contained 390 days, about 25 days more than the actual length of the year. Then they established a week consisting of 7 days. Each

22

day was named after one of their 7 gods and set aside for the worship of that particular god.

Each day and night was divided into 12-hour periods, so that every day-night interval consisted of 24 hours. They then conceived the idea of dividing each hour into 60 minutes, and each minute into 60 seconds. They could have measured seconds on a large sundial. Modern timepieces still use these divisions. Next time you glance at your watch, remember that its development can be traced back thousands of years to these ancient priests.

The Babylonian calendar of 360 days was about 5 days too short, for, as we know, the year consists of approximately 365¼ days. Every 6 years it would be wrong by 30 days, or 1 of their months. They solved the problem by simply doubling 1 month every sixth year, making the year 13 months long instead of 12. The process of inserting days or months into the calendar is known as *intercalation*.

The Babylonians are also credited with having devised the *zodiac,* by means of which they practiced *astrology.* This should not be confused with *astronomy,* which is a modern science concerned with the classification of knowledge based on verifiable laws. Astrology is a pseudo-science, which deals with such things as fortune-telling and the prediction of events to come.

The zodiac is an imaginary belt in the heavens which

23

swings through a full circle of 360 degrees and follows the apparent path of the sun. It is divided into 12 equal sections, each 30 degrees wide. Different constellations are visible in each section during each month of the year. The sections originally were named after the constellations they encompassed in Babylonian times. Since the positions of the earth and sun with respect to these stars has changed during the last 3,000 years, the constellations in these sections are quite different today.

The priests made a lucrative business out of telling fortunes and casting horoscopes. The people of that time attached great importance to their predictions and relied upon them for guidance in all of their affairs. For example, they consulted the priests before undertaking business deals, in order to find out which day would be most likely to bring them success. The priests would obtain the birth date of the person for whom the horoscope was to be cast, and then consult their sky charts and maps to determine the positions of the heavenly bodies on that day. After considerable study and "magic" ritual, they would report their findings. Certain days would be deemed lucky while others were to be avoided, for the sun and planets would not be in a favorable position. Even the king relied upon the pronouncements of his priest-astrologers, and would not undertake anything of importance without obtaining their approval.

24

While many people may regard all of this as unscientific mumbo jumbo, we must remember that the ancients took it all very seriously. As far as they were concerned, the priests were the interpreters of the gods, who, as heavenly bodies, could plainly be seen in the sky. Their advice was followed without question.

The zodiac served another purpose. The priests knew that each constellation occupied a certain position in

25

the sky at exactly the same time each year. This served as a check on their lunar calendar and enabled them to make their corrections at the proper time.

The Babylonian astrologers also made a specialty of predicting future events. Since they were clever businessmen, as well as trained celestial observers, we may be sure that they played the game safely and foretold only those events of which they could be fairly certain. Their knowledge of astronomy made it possible for them to predict eclipses of the sun and the moon. They had also discovered the influence of the sun and the moon upon the tides, and they must have acquired considerable skill in predicting unusual weather conditions.

These Babylonian priests earned such a reputation for their skill at magic and astronomy that for many years afterward astrologers were known as Babylonians or Chaldeans. Even today, the traditional picture of an astrologer is that of a bearded man, dressed in a robe and wearing a tall, pointed (Babylonian) hat.

LUNAR CALENDARS

Other civilizations developed their own calendars. Most of these made use of lunar months—the time it took for the moon to go through its phases. The Babylonians had reckoned the lunar month as having 30 days

26

but this was later changed to 29½ days. Since it was impossible to have a 29½-day month, alternate months of 29 and 30 days were established. Thus, the average length of each month was 29½ days.

A year consisting of 12 lunar months had 354 days. Since the solar year has approximately 365¼ days, the lunar year was short by about 11¼ days. These missing days were intercalated, or added to the calendar in order to match the number of days in the solar year.

HISTORIC CALENDARS

Greek

The early Greeks used a lunar calendar. Instead of adding 11¼ days each year, they added 90 days every 8 years, in the form of 3 intercalary 30-day months.

Egyptian

The ancient Egyptians originally devised a lunar calendar, but eventually discarded it in favor of a solar calendar. This was based upon the apparent movement of the sun, rather than lunar months. They used 12 months of 30 days each, with 5 extra days added each year. This brought the total number of days to 365, which was about ¼ of a day too short. In 238 B.C., King

27

Ptolemy III adjusted the calendar by adding a day every fourth year. This calendar was very similar to the solar calendar we consult today.

The Egyptian astronomers checked the accuracy of their calendar by observing the annual appearance of the Dog Star, Sirius, above the horizon, which occurred on the same day each year.

Chinese

No one knows exactly when the Chinese invented their lunar calendar, but we do know that as early as 2000 B.C. they were improving the one which was then in use. They used a system of 24 half-months, and a year of 365 days. The solar and lunar years were reconciled by adding 7 months every 19 years. However, discrepancies still existed; the equinoxes did not always fall on the same day, and the years were not always the same length. In the seventeenth century, at the request of the emperor, the calendar was revised and corrected by Jesuit missionaries. It remained in use until 1911, when the imperial government was overthrown. In 1912 the Chinese Republic adopted the Gregorian calendar, which was used by all the Western countries. Despite this, most of the people continued to use the ancient calendar until it was officially forbidden in 1930.

28

Mohammedan

In A.D. 622, when the prophet Mohammed was driven from Mecca, he fled to Medina. This flight is known as the Hegira, and marks the year *one* in the Mohammedan calendar. Prior to that time, the Arabs had used a lunar calendar with intercalations. When Mohammed assumed power, he revised the calendar so that the year had 12 lunar months of 29 and 30 days alternately, and consisted of 354 days. Intercalations were forbidden, probably because of former abuses of the old calendar. No attempt was made to lengthen the calendar year, even though it was about 11¼ days shorter than the solar year. This calendar is still in use.

As a result, the Moslem months occur 11¼ days earlier each year and have no connection with the seasons, which are disregarded. Holidays are celebrated on fixed calendar days. Every 32½ years they move completely backward through the seasons.

There are about 33 Moslem years to every 32 of ours.

Hebrew

The Hebrew calendar is of ancient origin. It begins with the year 3761 B.C., which is considered the time of the Creation. In order to find the approximate Hebrew equivalent of any year in the Gregorian calendar, the

29

one we use, simply add 3761. Our year 1957 corresponds to the Hebrew year 5718. The year 2000 will be 5761 according to the Hebrew calendar. The exact month cannot be determined in the same manner, as the Hebrew new year occurs around the autumnal equinox, September 23, while our new year, January 1, is in midwinter.

The Hebrew calendar consists of 12 lunar months, of 30 and 29 days, alternately. Unlike the Mohammedan calendar, which is purely lunar in character, it is adjusted to the solar year by means of intercalations. These follow a 19-year cycle; a 29-day month is intercalated 7 times every 19 years. It is the oldest of all the calendars in use today.

Mayan

The ancient Mayas had no way of communicating with the Old World. Yet they achieved a cultural level which in many ways surpassed anything known in the world at the time. They developed an original system of writing which they carved on square stone columns called *steles*. They also wrote in books made of strips of paper-like tree bark, which were cemented together with natural gums. They developed a form of mathematics which they used in complicated astronomical calculations; in this concept they were many hundreds of years ahead of the best European mathematicians.

The Mayan calendar was truly remarkable. Through the years it underwent a series of changes, eventually emerging as an amazingly accurate device. It provided for 18 months of 20 days each, with a 5-day period at the end. The Mayan calendar year was found to be the same as the Gregorian year. Interestingly enough, their astronomers developed essentially the same instruments for observing the heavens as those used by the ancient Chinese, Babylonians and Egyptians.

Roman

Our present calendar is derived from the one developed by the Romans. The earliest Roman calendar had 10 months, totaling 304 days. The months did not have an equal number of days; 5 months had 31 days, 4 months had 30 days, and 1 month had 29 days. The new year always began on March 1. About 713 B.C., King Numa is said to have added Januarius and Februarius to the calendar, giving the year 12 months, and a total of 355 days.

The months were arranged in their present order by the Decemvirs, a group of ten officials, who were given the power to formulate a new body of laws. The change

31

was made about 451 B.C.; at this time Januarius was made the first month of the year.

Soon after 200 B.C., the regulation of the calendar was placed in the hands of the *pontifex maximus,* the official head of the Roman religion. According to tradition, days were frequently removed from or added to the calendar in order to shorten or lengthen the terms of certain officials. This led to a very confusing state of affairs, for no one could tell in advance exactly how long the year was likely to be. This political abuse of the calendar went on until the time of Julius Caesar, when it was found that January occurred in autumn—3 months out of date!

Julian

In 46 B.C. Julius Caesar became *pontifex maximus.* In response to continued complaints about the calendar he decided to bring about a sweeping reform. Aided by Sosigines, an Alexandrian astronomer, he devised a plan whereby the months of the year would be brought into their proper relation to the seasons.

The calendar was brought up to date by lengthening the year 46 B.C., so that it contained 445 days. This was done by inserting 3 intercalary months. A 23-day month was placed after Februarius, and 2 months of 34

32

and 33 days were added between November and December; as a result, the spring of 45 B.C. began at the proper time, in March. This step had another result: It so bewildered the methodical Romans, that thereafter they referred to 46 B.C. as the "year of confusion."

Next, the length of the solar year was determined to be 365¼ days. Normal years were to be 365 days long. Every fourth year an intercalary day was to be added to Februarius, in order to correct the calendar.

The use of lunar months was abandoned completely and the length of the new months altered. With the exception of February, they were given either 31 or 30 days. Februuary had 29 days during normal years and 30 during leap years. The name of the month Quintilis was changed to July, in honor of Julius Caesar. The calendar became known as the Julian calendar.

The Romans did not number each day of the month as we do. Instead, they counted from three days: the Kalends, the Nones and the Ides. The Kalends were the first day of each month. The Nones were the seventh day in March, May, July and October; in the other months they fell on the fifth day. The Ides were the fifteenth of March, May, July and October; in the other months they corresponded to the thirteenth day. When the soothsayer in Shakespeare's play, *Julius Caesar,* warned, "Beware the Ides of March," he was referring

33

☽ MOHAMMEDAN

29 DAYS	30	29	30	29	3

☽ HEBREW

30 DAYS	29	30	29	30

☀ MAYAN

20	20	20	20	20	20	20	20

☀ JULIAN

31 DAYS	28 or 29	31	30	31	

☀ GREGORIAN   SUPPRESS

31 DAYS	28 or 29	31	30	31	

to the fifteenth day of the month of March. Had he said "Beware the Ides of April," he would have meant April thirteenth.

Days were counted *before* the Kalends, Nones, o Ides. For example, August 28 was the fifth day befor the Kalends of September, and was therefore called th fifth Kalends of September. From the Kalends, day were reckoned backward to the Ides, or the thirteentl of August. Days between the Ides and the Nones wer counted back from the Ides. This meant that a Roman speaking of the date we know as August 10, would refe to the fourth Ides of August. Continuing in the sam manner, days between the Nones and the Kalends wer counted back from the Nones.

354 DAYS

| 30 | 29 | 30 | 29 | 30 |

WITH 19-YEAR CYCLE INTERCALATIONS

| 29 | 30 | 29 | 30 | 29 |

365 DAYS

| 20 | 20 | 20 | 20 | 20 | 20 | 20 | 20 | 5 |

365 DAYS

| 31 | 30 | 31 | 30 | 31 |

YEAR ON CENTURY YEARS NOT DIVISIBLE BY 400

| 31 | 30 | 31 | 30 | 31 |

During leap year, the intercalary day added to February was always inserted between the twenty-third and twenty-fourth day of the month. Despite this added day, February 23 was always known as the seventh Kalends of March. This created an interesting situation, for now there were 2 days reckoned as the sixth Kalends. Because of this, the Julian leap year is technically known as a *bissextile* (Latin-twice sixth) year.

During the reign of Augustus, who ascended to power after the death of Julius Caesar, several minor changes were made in the calendar. They did not affect the length of the calendar, nor did they change its essential character.

35

Sextilis, the sixth month in the old Latin calendar, was renamed August, in honor of the Emperor Augustus. One day was taken away from February and added to August, so that it would have the same number of days as July, which had been named for Julius Caesar. September and November were reduced to 30 days; the days taken from these months were added to October and December, which now had 31. There is some doubt as to whether these last changes were introduced by Julius or Augustus. At any rate, the months were given the number of days that they have at the present time.

Gregorian

The Julian year was 365 days and 6 hours long, which is 11 minutes and 14 seconds longer than the true length of the solar year. This difference was not immediately apparent, but its effect was noted eventually. Every year, the calendar gained 11 minutes and 14 seconds; every 128 years, it gained a full day. This went on until the sixteenth century, by which time the calendar had gained 10 days. As a result, the vernal equinox occurred on March 21 instead of March 11.

Unless something could be done to remedy the situation, the discrepancy between the calendar dates and the seasons would increase until, as in the old Roman calendar, they would have no relation to each other.

Calendar reform was undertaken by Pope Gregory XIII. In 1582, he announced two major alterations of the Julian calendar. The result was the Gregorian calendar, which is used at the present time. First, the year 1582 was to be shortened by 10 days, in order to restore the spring equinox to its proper place in the calendar. This was accomplished by abolishing the 10 days following October 4, 1582. Quite simply, by a stroke of the pen, the day following October 4 became October 15.

Next, the length of the calendar year had to be altered so that it matched the solar year as closely as possible. The system of a leap year every fourth year was retained, with one difference: only those century years which could be evenly divided by 400 were to be leap years. The year 1600, divisible by 400 ($1600 \div 400 = 4$), was a leap year, but 1700, 1800 and 1900 were not. The year 2000 will be a leap year.

The solar year is decreasing in length by about 0.53 seconds a century. This, plus the very small error (26 seconds per year) in the Gregorian calendar will eventually cause a discrepancy between the calendar and the solar year. It has been estimated that the calendar will be about one day ahead of the solar year by the year 4000.

France, Italy, Spain and Portugal, the Catholic countries of Europe, adopted the Gregorian calendar at once. It was put to use in the Catholic German states in 1584, but the Protestant Germans continued to use the Julian calendar until 1700. Other Protestant countries were even slower to accept it. Great Britain kept the Old Style (Julian) calendar until 1752, by which time a difference of 11 days existed between England and the New Style (Gregorian) calendar of continental Europe. When the new calendar was adopted, the beginning of the year was changed from Annunciation Day, March 25, to January 1. At the same time, the calendar was brought up to date by dropping 11 days, so that September 2 was followed immediately by September 14.

This last move was resented bitterly by many Englishmen. Riots spread throughout the country as people demanded the return of their 11 days. Workmen claimed wages for the missing days; others objected because they felt the adoption of the Gregorian calendar was a "return to popery." The matter became an issue in local elections. William Hogarth, the famous contemporary political and social cartoonist, portrayed a group of people shouting, "Give us back our eleven days!" Poems were written attacking the new calendar, and the controversy raged far and wide.

38

However, the Gregorian calendar was officially adopted by Parliament, and eventually the clamor died down.

French Revolutionary Calendar

An interesting development took place during the French Revolution when the National Convention, in its violent hatred of anything symbolic of the old regime, abolished the Gregorian Calendar. The new official calendar dated from the proclamation of the Republic in 1792, but actually went into effect almost a year later. It provided for 12 months of 30 days, with 5 added feast days, called *sans-culottides*. These were named in honor of the brave but impoverished citizens of Paris who could not afford knee breeches (*culottes*). They fought behind street barricades in long trousers or other improvised garments. This scheme was identical to the one used in ancient Egypt.

The names of the months were fanciful, and represented a complete break with tradition:

Vendémiaire	(*vintage month*)	Germinal	(*seed*)
Brumaire	(*fog*)	Floréal	(*blossom*)
Frimaire	(*frost*)	Prairial	(*pasture*)
Nivôse	(*snow*)	Messidor	(*harvest*)
Pluviôse	(*rain*)	Thermidor	(*heat*)
Ventôse	(*wind*)	Fructidor	(*fruit*)

Traditional weeks were abolished. Instead, the months were divided into 3 10-day periods, or *decades;* every tenth day was a holiday. Sundays and religious festivals no longer existed.

If France had been able to exist isolated from the rest of the world, this calendar might have remained in effect indefinitely. However, relations with other countries had to be maintained, and since they all used the Gregorian calendar the French calendar was found to be a cumbersome instrument. In 1805, Napoleon restored the Gregorian calendar.

Sixty-six years later, the citizens of Paris revived the Revolutionary Calendar. Toward the close of the Franco-Prussian War, the Parisians had resisted the Germans to the bitter end, withstanding constant bombardment and a siege of five months. Finally, faced with starvation, they yielded. Their fierce resentment of the national government's agreement to a humiliating peace with Prussia soon led to one of the bloodiest periods in the history of France. Once again Paris was besieged, this time by Frenchmen, under the authority of the Versailles government. A communal form of government was set up in the city, and for two months the calendar of the old Revolution was back in use. After a week of desperate street fighting, Paris surrendered; the calendar died with the revolt.

40

CALENDAR REFORM

Even though the Gregorian calendar is the most accurate one that has ever been widely used, it has a number of inherent faults:

1. We have two types of year, and they are not the same length; common years contain 365 days, leap years, 366.

2. The calendar cannot be evenly divided into half years, quarter years, months, or weeks. A quarter year may contain 90, 91, or 92 days.

3. The months are irregular in length; they may contain 28, 29, 30, or 31 days.

4. Months are not evenly divisible by weeks. Weeks often begin in one month, and extend into the next.

5. Years begin on different days of the week.

6. Holidays fall on any day of the week.

These and other calendar irregularities are the cause of much unnecessary difficulty in business. Such things as salaries, taxes and vital statistics could be computed very simply if the year could be divided into periods of equal length.

Various organizations have been established to reform the calendar, and many solutions have been offered. Among the ideas that have found supporters is that of the Thirteen-Month Calendar. This has a year consist-

41

ing of 13 months, each exactly 4 weeks long. The months retain their present names and arrangement; the thirteenth month, to be called *Sol,* is inserted between June and July. The extra day added during leap year is added to Sol. The last day of each year is a *year day,* and does not belong to any month or week. This scheme has certain advantages. Calendar irregularities are eliminated. New years always begin on Sunday and end on Saturday. The dates of each month always fall on the same day of the week; for example, the first, eighth, fifteenth and twenty-second of each month would always be Sundays.

The Thirteen-Month Calendar appears simple and logical, but it actually has some serious flaws. In the first place, its adoption would mean a complete rearrangement of our present calendar. All of our months would be reduced to 28 days, causing endless complications. Months which now have 30 days would lose 2 days, and 31-day months would lose 3.

In all, a total of 94 days would have to be moved out of place into other months. In other words, slightly more than 25 per cent of the days of the year would be shifted to other months! This would amount to a complete dislocation of our system of dating events. One-quarter of the people of the world would have to learn new dates for their birthdays, anniversaries and holidays. People born on January 29 would find that it no longer existed

42

and that they had been arbitrarily switched to February 1!

It is true that a 13-month year has one advantage: the months have an equal number of days. However, a year consisting of 13 months cannot be divided into equal halves or quarters containing full months: $13 \div 2 = 6\frac{1}{2}$; $13 \div 4 = 3\frac{1}{4}$. The business world would have to set up new systems of accounting and abandon those present ones which make use of the half-year and quarter-year.

The chief objection to the Thirteen-Month Calendar lies in the fact that our present calendar would have to be completely discarded.

Another calendar-reform movement which has won the support of many groups advocates the adoption of the World Calendar. A year of 364 days is used as the basis for reckoning time. A Year-End Day and an added day during leap year bring the calendar into harmony with the length of the solar year.

The year is divided into 4 equal quarters of 91 days. This is an improvement over the Gregorian calendar, in which the quarter-years may have 90, 91, or 92 days.

The twelve months are retained in their present order. Each quarter is composed of 3 months, arranged as follows:

43

WHEEL OF TIME

First Quarter:	January	31 days
	February	30 days
	March	30 days
Second Quarter:	April	31 days
	May	30 days
	June	30 days
Third Quarter:	July	31 days
	August	30 days
	September	30 days
Fourth Quarter:	October	31 days
	November	30 days
	December	30 days

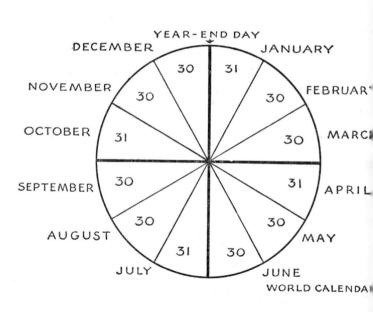

The number of days in each month has been changed so that the 4 quarters are identical in structure; they each contain exactly 13 weeks. Notice that each quarter begins with a 31-day month, and is followed by 2 months of 30 days. The days are arranged so that each quarter begins with a Sunday and ends with a Saturday.

Unlike the Thirteen-Month Calendar, which moved 94 days out of place, the World Calendar calls for shifting only 8 days. This does not involve a very serious dislocation of our present calendar. Many people feel that this change can be easily accomplished. Proponents of the plan point out the following advantages:

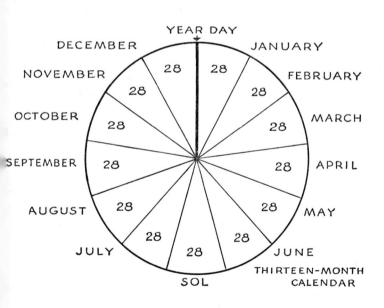

1. The calendar would not have to be changed from year to year, since the days of each month would be fixed.

2. The number of days in each month would be more equal than they are at present. Instead of months having 28, 29, 30, or 31 days, months would contain either 30 or 31 days.

3. Half-years and quarter-years would be equalized. This would simplify accounting.

Perhaps one day such a calendar may be adopted. Of course, it would require the co-operation of all the nations of the world. Such a move could conceivably be carried out by a world organization such as the United Nations. Will the Gregorian calendar be changed? Time will tell.

3

HOURS AND MINUTES

WE have said that primitive man's first clock was the sun. He watched it move across the heavens each day and eventually learned to reckon time by tallying the number of times it rose and set. One day he noticed that shadows cast by the sun, seemed to move also and an idea was born.

We can well imagine what happened next. As the sun rose in the east one morning, it caused a tree stump or vertical slab of stone to cast a shadow toward the west. As the sun moved, so did the shadow. It crept gradually around in a semicircle until evening, when it pointed toward the east. Man's next step was to mark different positions of the shadow during the day. He might have done this by simply scratching marks in the earth or placing stones on the ground as markers. This simple discovery created the first timepiece.

The first, regular, man-made time divisions were un-

47

doubtedly worked out as a matter of necessity. In those early days, men had to stand guard against numerous enemies. Since night represented the time of greatest danger, it was probably divided into periods at which the guard was changed. These guard periods became known as *watches*. Later, the word "watch" came to mean as well any definite period of time during the day or night.

The Old Testament makes frequent mention of watches, for the ancient Hebrews divided day and night into 3 periods each. Their time periods were arranged something like this:

Ancient	*Modern*
Day	
First Watch	sunrise to mid-morning
Second Watch	mid-morning to mid-afternoon
Third Watch	mid-afternoon to sunset
Night	
First Watch	sunset to midnight
Second Watch	midnight to about 3:00 A.M.
Third Watch	3:00 A.M. to sunrise

Later, during the time of the New Testament, day and nights were each divided into 4 equal watches.

48

More than 6,000 years ago, the Egyptians of the Early Kingdom divided their day into 12 hours. The Chinese used the same idea as far back as 2700 B.C., and, later, the Greeks also divided day and night into 12 hours each.

In all of the ancient systems, the time divisions were merely equal divisions of day or night. Since days and nights became shorter or longer at different times of the year, the watches or hours also became shorter or longer.

The idea of using hours of equal length was introduced in the thirteenth century by Abul Hassan, an Arabian mathematician and astronomer. He calculated the length of 1 hour as $\frac{1}{12}$ of the period of daylight at one of the equinoxes, when day and night are of equal length. This created a day of 24 hours.

When primitive man first marked the path of a moving shadow, he had no idea that he was taking the first step toward developing the science of horology. Horology (Greek = *hora,* or hour) is concerned with the measurement of time, or the construction of time-measuring or recording instruments.

Soon other inventive minds devised improvements over the first crude shadow clocks. Tree stumps and rock slabs were replaced by shadow sticks, straight rods which were driven into the ground. The use of shadow sticks led to the invention of the sundial.

49

THE SUNDIAL

The sundial was essentially a simple device. It consisted of a rod, or pointer, called a *gnomon,* which was
fastened in place so that it cast a shadow upon a flat
surface, or *dial*. The dial was marked off to show hours
and, later, minutes.

The sundial first came into use so long ago that we
can only guess its origin. The earliest existing sundial
was found in Egypt and dates back to 1500 B.C. For the
earliest literary reference to sundials, we turn once again
to the Bible. About 700 B.C., the prophet Isaiah spoke
of "the sundial of Ahaz."

Practically all of the world's great civilizations used
the sundial. It took many different forms but was constructed along the same basic lines. Some authorities
believe that the Egyptian pyramids were used in reckoning time. Obelisks, such as Cleopatra's Needle, which
is now in Central Park, New York City, may have been
designed as gnomons for immense sundials.

In some countries cruder forms of the sundial were
devised. Sometimes a hole would be placed in the roof
of a structure in such a manner that a beam of light would
be admitted to the interior. As the day progressed
spot of light would move across the walls.

About 240 B.C., Berossos, a priest-astronomer of

Chaldea, invented an interesting variation of the sundial. Instead of a flat dial, he used a hemisphere resembling one half of a hollow ball. The gnomon extended horizontally and cast a shadow inside the hemisphere, which was marked off to show the hours. This device became known as the Hemicycle of Berossos and was used for hundreds of years. Both the hemicycle and the hemisphere (like the Paul dial, page 53), a variation, were in great demand in Greece and Rome.

Once the principle of the sundial became known, it began to appear in a wide variety of sizes and shapes. Large dials were situated in public places. Smaller models adorned gardens, and still smaller, portable types were carried in purses or worn as bracelets. One very popular model was a ring, the inside of which was

51

cleverly engraved so that when it was held vertically a beam of sunlight came through a tiny hole in the top and indicated the time.

An improvement in the design of sundials occurred about the first century A.D., when it was found that setting the gnomon parallel to the earth's axis resulted in greater accuracy. This was done by pointing it toward the North Star.

We must not think that the sundial vanished with ancient times. It remained in common use for many centuries. As the science of mathematics developed, the accuracy of sundials was improved. It became possible to calculate precise markings with the aid of trigonometry. Many books were written on the subject some of which presented simplified formulas and directions, so that the average man could lay out his own dial markings. It was only as recently as the eighteenth century that sundials declined in popularity due to the widespread use of clocks and watches. And even then they were not completely abandoned. As a matter of fact they were frequently consulted as a check on the accuracy of the very clocks and watches which had taken their place as timekeepers.

The sundial had several defects which made it an unsatisfactory instrument for modern timekeeping. It first fault was that it measured solar time, dividing each period of daylight into 12 hours. This would be perfect if all our daylight periods were of equal length, but of course they aren't. The length of each daylight period varies with the seasons. We all know that days are longer during the summer than they are in the winter. Since the sundial made no distinction between summer and winter, the hours it showed during summer were longer than those indicated during winter.

There was another more serious flaw in the sundial. Our days are not uniform in length. We think of each day as having exactly 24 hours but, with the exception of 4 days during the year, they may be shorter or longer.

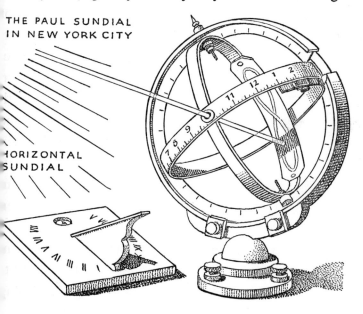

THE PAUL SUNDIAL
IN NEW YORK CITY

HORIZONTAL
SUNDIAL

Discrepancies range from a few seconds to as much as 16 minutes. The average, or *mean* length of all the days of the year is 24 hours. For this reason, time shown on a sundial will almost always be slow or fast when compared with an accurate clock, which shows hours of absolutely uniform length.

Sundials could be referred to only during the day, and even then had to be read outdoors. They were useless on dark or rainy days or in deeply shaded places. They were of no value to travelers, for they would give erroneous readings when removed from the latitude for which they had been designed. They were useless on board ship since the slightest motion would cause the shadow of the pointer to swing about on the dial.

THE WATER CLOCK

The sundial was not the only timekeeping device available in the ancient world. At least 5,000 years ago the Chinese are said to have used the *clepsydra,* or water clock, but this has never been proven. It is generally considered an invention of the Egyptians, who describe its construction about 2000 B.C. From Egypt, the use of the clepsydra spread to Greece and Rome.

The clepsydra was a simple instrument. In its earliest form it probably consisted of a vessel of water, with

54

small opening in the bottom through which the water dripped. The rate at which the water escaped could be controlled by making the hole larger or smaller. The inside of the vessel was marked off into 24 divisions. As the water level dropped inside the vessel, it reached the different markings showing the time.

In India another simple type was used. This was merely a small bowl through which a tiny hole had been drilled. When set into a larger vessel containing water, it gradually filled and sank. Marks inside the bowl indicated the time.

Some water clocks were designed as vessels containing a float. These vessels were marked off in divisions to indicate hours. When water dripped into the vessel, the water level rose and the float rose with it. Other types depended upon the downward movement of the float as water ran out of the container.

As interest in accurate timekeeping developed, it became apparent that the clepsydra needed improvement. It was noticed that clepsydrae tended to slow down as the water escaped. When the water level dropped, the water pressure within the vessel lessened and the water ran out more slowly. This was solved by using two containers of water. One was kept completely filled, so that the water would run out under the same pressure at all times. This dripped into the second container. which

55

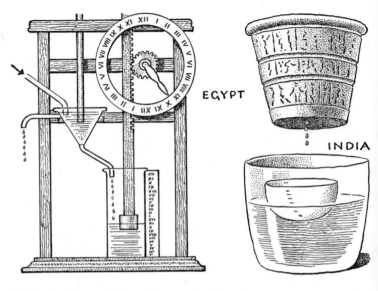

EGYPT

INDIA

held the float. Since it received water at an even rate, the rising float could show time accurately.

It wasn't long before man's inventive mind began to devise ways of putting this water power to use in order to create a more efficient instrument for telling time. Why not wind a cord around an axle and attach the other end to the float? As the float rose in the water vessel, the cord would unwind and cause the axle to turn. A pointer attached to one end of the axle would indicate the hours on a dial. Or, why not equip a float with a set of teeth so that they could engage a gear? The rising float would make the gear turn, and this could be used to power any number of mechanical devices. These ideas must surely have occurred to Ctesibius, a mechanical genius who lived in Alexandria in the second century B.C. He is credited with having been the first to construct a clepsydra which used toothed wheels.

Water clocks were used in the law courts of Athens and Rome to show the time allotted to speakers. Writers of that time indicate that unscrupulous Roman lawyers would attempt to slow up the clocks in order to gain more time. Given the opportunity, they would interfere with the mechanism, or even throw foreign matter into the water to prevent it from running out rapidly.

The clepsydra was the common man's timepiece for hundreds of years and was abandoned only when the use of mechanical clocks became widespread. Most of them were very simple affairs which possessed no moving parts. They were often made in the form of a tall, hollow metal tube; a tiny hole in the bottom caused it to fill and sink when it was placed in a larger container of water. Some of these were constructed to show the hours for an entire day. However, centuries ago people weren't concerned about the time during the night, so the clepsydrae were usually emptied and placed in operation each morning. Clepsydrae of this type were widely used in Europe until about the beginning of the sixteenth century.

57

Not all water clocks were simple in design. Many had complicated mechanical features and were cleverly designed to show the hours in various ways. Some even had striking mechanisms, by means of which a bell or gong was sounded. Here were the forerunners of our modern alarm clocks!

Long ago, it was customary for rulers of nations to send each other costly gifts as tokens of good faith and esteem. Harun-al-Rashid, the celebrated Caliph of the *Arabian Nights,* was a great patron of the arts and sciences. Under his rule, Baghdad became the cultural center of the East. He communicated with Charlemagne, the Emperor of the West and, in the year 807, sent him a gift which reflected the splendor of his court. This was a clepsydra, elaborately wrought in bronze and gold. The dial had 12 doors, each of which represented an hour. At the stroke of each hour, a door opened and the proper number of small metal balls dropped onto a brass bell. At 12 o'clock, a figure of a horseman appeared in each door, after which they all closed.

The clepsydra had several advantages over the sundial. For one thing, its operation did not depend upon the sun. For this reason, it could be adjusted to show mean time instead of solar time and could indicate hours of equal length. It could be used indoors or outdoors, and it kept time at the same steady rate both day and

58

night. The same clepsydra could be used to show time in any part of the world, since it was not affected by changes in latitude. Furthermore, it kept accurate time.

The clepsydra was by no means a perfect timekeeper. Like the sundial, it could not be used on shipboard. Many types required constant attention because the vessel which supplied water to the time-recording float had to be kept filled to overflowing at all times. Since all clepsydrae operated by means of water, they were not suited for portable use. The very fact that the clepsydra depended upon water for its operation prohibited its use in freezing weather; if the water froze, the clock would stop. However, despite its faults, the clepsydra was for many years the best instrument known for telling time.

THE HOURGLASS

This is another ancient timekeeper. The date of its invention and its place of origin are unknown. Liutprand, a Carthusian monk of the eighth century A.D., is believed by some to have invented the hourglass, but this is purely legendary, as the device appeared in Greek sculpture as far back as 250 B.C.

The hourglass worked in a simple manner. It consisted of two funnel-shaped glass bulbs, connected by a narrow neck and fixed in a frame so that one was directly

59

above the other. The bulb on top contained a quantity of fine sand which would run down into the other bulb in exactly one hour. At the end of that time, the hourglass was reversed and the process was repeated. Some early glasses contained mercury instead of sand, but they were not entirely satisfactory.

Hourglasses were common in Europe during the Middle Ages and remained popular until about the middle of the seventeenth century. They are pictured in the works of many famous artists, and it is interesting to see how they were employed. Albrecht Dürer's wood engraving, "Saint Jerome in His Study" shows an hour-

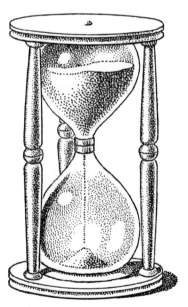

glass on a shelf. A woodcut in a book published in Florence in 1500 shows an hourglass used in a classroom where a lecturer is addressing his pupils. Hans Holbein used the hourglass to symbolize the passing of time, in his woodcut series, "The Dance of Death."

The idea of the hourglass as a symbol of time's passing was accepted throughout Europe. Glasses were placed in coffins, to show that time had indeed run out for the one who had died. Poets have alluded so often to the "sands of time," that the phrase needs no explanation. Continuing in the same grim vein, we are all familiar with the picture of Father Time, an old man who carries a scythe—and an hourglass.

Hourglasses worked on the same principle as the clepsydra, in that both measured something that ran from one container to another. However, an hourglass did not require constant attention; it could be stood on end and there it would remain until it was time to reverse it. Unlike the clepsydra, it did not have to be refilled; it was a self-contained mechanism that never needed regulation or adjustment. One of its great advantages was that it could not freeze and thus could be used in any climate. The sand ran at a steady rate, no matter what the temperature might be.

Because it was practically foolproof, the hourglass was for centuries the only device that could keep fair

61

time on board ships. A member of the crew, usually a cabin boy, had the job of turning the glass regularly. The British navy used half-hour and one-hour glasses until well into the nineteenth century.

Glasses were also made for special purposes. In the early days of sailing ships, a 28-second glass was used to calculate the speed of the vessel. In order to do this, a piece of wood called a *log chip* was fastened to one end of a *log line,* a thin rope with knots placed at intervals of 47 feet, 3 inches. The chip was thrown overboard, where it dragged and exerted a pull upon the line. The seaman who held the line counted the number of knots that passed through his hands in exactly 28 seconds. If he counted 10 knots, that was the ship's speed; thus, we have the origin of the *knot,* as used to indicate nautical speed. This worked upon a simple principle: 47 feet, 3 inches are to 1 nautical mile (6,080.20 feet) as 28 seconds are to 1 hour. Counting knots was the same as counting nautical miles per hour.

People found a great variety of uses for the hourglass. Until the middle of the seventeenth century it was the custom to time the length of sermons with an hourglass; the practice still continues in some churches today. As a matter of fact, we use glasses in our daily lives. Some people use 5-minute glasses to time telephone calls,

and many a soft-boiled egg has been prepared while the sands ran out in a 3-minute glass.

FIRE CLOCKS

Man's efforts to perfect timekeeping devices even led him to experiment with fire. The time it took for a log to be consumed may well have been one of the earliest time measurements. However, this was obviously an uncertain method, for some kinds of wood burned more rapidly than others. Besides, the condition of the wood influenced the speed with which it burned; it might smolder when wet and blaze up quickly if dry. A search began for some substance that would burn at a regular, predictable rate.

The ancient Chinese produced a wick which was knotted at regular intervals. Lighted at one end, it slowly smoldered from knot to knot, the distance between the knots indicating the time. They also burned cylinders composed of glue and sawdust or pitch and sawdust. These, too, were designed to mark the hours. The Japanese used the same contrivances.

Roman inventiveness produced the lamp clock, which not only provided light but also showed the time. This consisted of a long glass tube which was sealed at the bottom and set in a vertical position. It was marked along its length with numbers which indicated the hours. Oil was poured into the tube, exactly up to the mark that represented the hour at which it was being filled. The oil was then lighted. As the oil was consumed, its level within the tube dropped, showing the time as it reached the different marks. Lamp clocks remained in use throughout the centuries, particularly in backward rural areas. Some European peasants depended upon clocks of this type until well after the beginning of the twentieth century.

After candles were invented, it was inevitable that they be put to use as timekeepers. This was done by simply noting the time it took for a candle of a given length and thickness to burn down completely. It was then a simple matter to divide a candle into equal parts by painting it with alternating bands of color. As the candle burned, each part consumed would represent a definite time interval, such as an hour, a half-hour, or less.

Legend attributes the invention of the candle clock to King Alfred the Great of England, who is said to have divided his day into three 8-hour periods; he devoted these periods to religion, public affairs, and recreation and rest.

If you would like to try something just for fun, you can improvise a candle clock very easily. First you must mark off your candle into equal divisions of about one inch. Then, light the candle and determine the rate at which it burns by timing it with a clock. All you have to do is find out how long it takes the candle to burn down one inch. You can then mark off divisions representing half and quarter hours. Candle clocks can be fairly accurate.

You can even make a candle alarm clock by sticking a pin into a candle at the proper place and suspending an object from the pin with a length of thread. When the candle burns down to the pin, the object will fall. If you choose something that makes enough noise when it falls, the alarm will work.

65

THE CLOCK

The clock was the first purely mechanical instrument for telling time. Its origins are shrouded in antiquity. No one man can be named as its inventor, for many contributed to its development.

Archimedes, the Greek mathematician, inventor and physicist, is believed to have invented a clock about 200 B.C. He is known to have constructed a machine which contained wheels and which depended upon a weight for its motive power. Very little is known about the details of the mechanism, but from all accounts it did not have a regulator or some other means of controlling the power imparted to it by the weight. It was certainly no more efficient than the water clocks of the time.

Other clock mechanisms have been attributed to Boethius, the Roman philosopher and statesman (510 A.D.), and Pacificus, the archdeacon of Verona (850 A.D.). Since no detailed descriptions of their works survive, most authorities are inclined to think that they merely developed different versions of the clepsydra.

The fall of the Roman empire in the fifth century marked the beginning of a period known as the Dark Ages. For the next 1,000 years, Europe remained cloaked in ignorance, superstition and intellectual dark-

66

ness. The literature and scientiflc achievements of Greece and Rome were forgotten and barbarism ruled. Invention was not only discouraged but punished, for anything that could not be understood by the ignorant people of that time was considered the work of Satan.

This was the period during which Christianity spread and took hold in Europe. Many monastic religious communities were founded, and it was in these that the feeble spark of learning was kept alive. Many of the monks knew Latin, but practically none of the common people could read or write. Such was the spirit of the times that most of the noblemen considered reading and writing to be effeminate and employed clerks to attend to their correspondence.

Despite the discouraging conditions that prevailed, some people with inventive and inquisitive minds were still to be found. One of these was a French monk named Gerbert, an outstanding scholar who wrote on theology, the natural sciences and mathematics. He achieved wide fame as a teacher, and later became Pope Sylvester II. It is generally believed that he constructed a clock about 990 A.D. Authorities are divided as to the nature of the mechanism. Some claim that it had weights, wheels and a regulating device, while others insist that it was nothing more than an improved sundial.

At any rate, whether or not Gerbert actually invented

67

a clock, other monks of the same period must certainly have been working on the idea, for it is definitely known that clocks appeared in monasteries by the eleventh century.

The names of the men who devised these first crude clocks are not known, and we shall never know who they were. In those days knowledge was passed on by word of mouth, from person to person. Written communications were sent only when matters of great importance were concerned. There was no governmental postal service. The only mail services in existence were those which had been organized by wealthy bankers or businessmen.

Communities were small and isolated. Men rarely left their native villages, and then only for very short trips. Whenever necessary, noblemen traveled from place to place with heavily armed escorts. This was an age of violence and bloodshed; robber bands made traveling hazardous and no roads were safe.

Thus, these early inventors remain unknown because of the nature of the times in which they lived and worked. It was quite possible for a man to become famous in his community yet be completely unknown a short distance away. This brings up an interesting question: how many men of the Dark Ages made important scientific discoveries which were never publicized and died with them? One day, perhaps, someone searching through ancient monastery records may find documentary proof of such accomplishments. Until then, we shall never know.

The first monastery clocks served a definite purpose: they summoned the monks to prayer. They had no faces or hands, but they did have striking mechanisms by means of which an alarm bell was sounded. This was the signal for tolling the monastery bells, which were heard far and wide. The people of that time regulated their lives according to the sound of these bells. At first, only a few monasteries and churches had clocks, but they all had bells. In accordance with an early papal decree, they were rung seven times every 24 hours. The times at which the bells were sounded became known as the seven canonical hours.

Crude as these early clocks were, they nonetheless represented a tremendous advance in the development of timekeeping, for they embodied the same constructional features as modern clocks.

How does a clock work? In a simple analysis, every clock must meet the following requirements:

1. It must have a source of motive power, or driving force, which makes it run.

2. This power must be reduced and transmitted to the time-indicating device in some way.

3. There must be some means of regulating the speed at which the mechanism runs.

4. The clock must indicate time, either by showing it in some way or by producing a sound.

The first abbey clocks were very simple in construction. Imagine a drum, around which a cable has been wound. The free end of the cable is attached to a weight. The force of gravity acts upon this weight, causing it to exert a downward pull which, in turn, causes the drum to revolve rapidly. The motive power will be expended within a short time and with full force. In order to reduce the motive power, the drum is therefore attached to a series of wheels, called the *train*. These act as reduction gears; they diminish the power of the motive force and feed a small amount of energy to the hands.

This, however, is not enough. Geared mechanisms had been known for centuries, but no one had yet been able to solve the problem of *regulating the speed* at which such mechanisms would run. Here, then, was the significant contribution of the first clocks: they had such a regulating device, called an *escapement*. By interrupting the fall of the weight at regular intervals, the escapement controlled the amount of power it delivered. The motive power was allowed to *escape* to the drum in a series of regular pulsations. Instead of spinning uncontrolledly, the train would turn slowly and evenly. The first escapements were crude, but they worked.

Once a regular source of power was applied to the train, it was a relatively simple matter to work out some device which would make a hammer strike a bell at given times.

These clocks were very large and very heavy. Sometimes it was necessary to use weights of more than 500 pounds! In order to provide enough distance for the weight to fall, clocks were installed high up in towers or church steeples. Appropriately, they were called *tower clocks*.

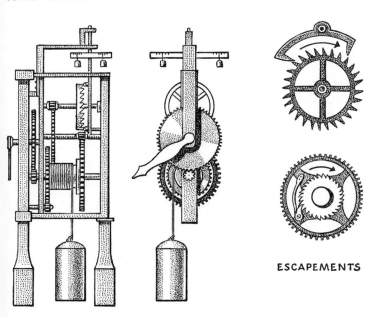

ESCAPEMENTS

Experiments and inventions progressed until a clock was developed which could strike each hour. Some of these clocks had complicated striking mechanisms, in which figures known as *Jacks* struck the hours on a bell. Grotesque figures and knights in armor were popular. In 1286, a clock was installed in the tower of St. Paul's Cathedral in London. The hours were struck by figures which became known as Paul's Jacks.

Dials began to appear on clocks. At first, these had only one hand which showed the hours. People had not yet begun to hurry in their daily lives, and minutes did not matter. Besides, clockmakers had yet to solve the problems involved in indicating minutes. Later, clocks were given two hands.

Clocks were installed in Westminster Hall in 1288, and in Canterbury Cathedral in 1292. Others began to appear in greater numbers in churches and public buildings. People no longer had to depend upon the sound of monastery bells, which tolled only the canonical hours. If they lived within sound of a clock, they could hear each hour struck.

Many clocks were built during the Middle Ages, but none was a really accurate timekeeper. As a matter of fact, they had to be adjusted to the correct time at regular intervals. Special caretakers were employed for this purpose; they were called *clock-setters*. As if to com-

72

pensate for their inaccuracy, clocks were endowed with all sorts of ingenious mechanical devices and lavish decorations. The craftsmen of medieval times were highly skilled, and in their clocks can be seen the same patient attention to intricate detail that is exhibited in the Gothic churches of the period.

The most famous of these complicated clocks is the one which was built by Isak Halbrecht and placed in the Cathedral of Strasbourg in 1352. This clock is three stories high and is a masterpiece of intricate mechanical construction. It was rebuilt twice, once in the sixteenth century, and again in the nineteenth century. On each occasion new features were added, so that it became a fantastically complex instrument. It contains a perpetual calendar, a celestial globe which shows the position of the sun, moon and stars, and mechanisms to show phases of the moon and eclipses of the sun. Automatic figures strike each hour. At noon, the figures of the three Magi bow before a statue of the Virgin, while a mechanical cock opens its beak, flaps its wings, ruffles its feathers, and crows. The clock has numerous other features as well. However, take away the figures and the intricate mechanical devices and what is left is a clock that doesn't even keep very good time. It is not nearly as accurate as a modern watch.

In 1364, King Charles V of France sent for Henry de Vick, a noted clockmaker of Württemberg, and commissioned him to build a clock for the tower of the royal palace (now the Palais de Justice) in Paris. De Vick accepted the assignment and set to work. The clock was completed in 1379—fifteen years after it was begun!

No wonder clocks of that time were rare. Imagine the cost of a clock which took fifteen years to build! Each clock was made specially for a particular place. Since there were no power machines, every part had to be fashioned by hand. Gears and pinions were patiently cut with a chisel and carefully fitted into the movement. If a clockmaker thought up an innovation in design, it might take him several years to make his idea workable.

Those who could afford them had clocks in their homes. These were miniatures of the tower clocks, and were also operated by weights. In order to provide enough height so that the weights would have room to descend, they were placed on high shelves. However, they kept time no better than the large clocks after which they were patterned. Clock mechanisms were often enclosed in intricately designed cases and richly ornamented.

Of the early clocks of that period, De Vick's is the one that most closely approaches those of modern times. Its escapement is of particular interest to us, for it used a rotating shaft called a *verge,* and a *foliot,* a balance arm by means of which the clock was regulated. Both the verge and the foliot remained in use in clocks for hundreds of years. Incidentally, De Vick's clock was keeping time in 1860—after almost 500 years of continuous service!

Men labored constantly to make clocks keep more accurate time. The craftsmen of the Middle Ages tinkered with their gears and wheels, but could not produce good timekeepers. As long as clocks depended upon weights for their motive power they could not be made portable. Until a better escapement could be designed, clocks would continue to run irregularly.

Men struggled with these problems for centuries. Then about the year 1500, Peter Henlein, a clockmaker of Nuremberg, invented a device which did away with the hanging weights. This was a straight spring, which was coiled. Upon unwinding, it furnished the motive power for the clock mechanism. The *mainspring,* as it came to be known, made it possible to construct small clocks which could be placed anywhere. Clocks no longer had to be bulky and heavy; lightweight types began to appear.

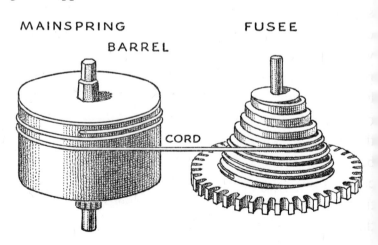

MAINSPRING BARREL   FUSEE   CORD

However, the adoption of the mainspring brought new problems to clockmakers. The mainspring was wound by means of a ratchet device, very much like the one used in clocks today. As it ran down, the amount of force it exerted upon the train of wheels decreased. The old foliot escapement was very sensitive to this changing force. It ran faster under increased pressure, and slowed down as the force decreased. Consequently, all clocks of this type slowed down as the mainspring unwound. People became quite adept at calculating the amount of time their clocks had lost at any given hour of the day. Clocks were still largely ornamental rather than practical, but they were fascinating mechanical gadgets and people were eager to own them.

About 1525, the problem of equalizing the mainspring's force was solved by Jacob Zech, a clockmaker of Prague, Bohemia, who invented the *fusee*. The fusee was a thick, cone-shaped wheel, with spiral grooves running around it. The mainspring was enclosed in a barrel, to which one end of a cord was attached. The rest of the cord was wound around the spiral grooves in the fusee. As the mainspring unwound, it turned the barrel, upon which the cord was slowly wound. This caused the cord to unwind from the fusee, at the same time making it turn. At first, the cord unwound from the small end of the fusee; as the mainspring ran down

77

and applied less force, the cord gradually exerted greater leverage upon the wide end of the fusee. In this way, the force of the mainspring was equalized, so that the power applied to the clock mechanism was the same at all times. This was a very important development in the science of clockmaking, and it left but one other major problem to be solved—that of designing an efficient escapement, so that clocks could be regulated to run more accurately.

By the sixteenth century, conditions in Europe were quite different from those of the Dark Ages. Many important developments had taken place during the preceding 400 years. The feudal system had disappeared, taking serfdom and armored knights with it. Great towns and cities had sprung up, dominated by beautiful Gothic churches. Trade had developed on an international scale, and merchant vessels sailed regularly from port to port.

Columbus had already discovered America, and Magellan had sailed around the world. Spain had embarked upon the greatest treasure hunt in history. The fabulous amount of gold and silver the Spaniards had plundered from their colonies in the New World had enabled that country to rise to world prominence for a brief time. This was the age when England emerged as a sea power, when Drake and Hawkins harassed

78

Spanish shipping and defeated the Great Armada. Shakespeare was writing his immortal plays, and England prospered under the rule of Queen Elizabeth.

The invention of printing, together with the introduction of paper from the East, had stimulated the production of cheap books. People no longer had to decipher monkish manuscripts written in Latin; now they could buy books printed in their own language. Reading, writing and learning were no longer confined to the monasteries. Schools and universities could be found throughout Europe, and intellectual activities flourished.

All over Europe, people were beginning to learn about the world in which they lived and were making attempts to solve its mysteries. They laid the foundations for the sciences of today. This was the time of Leonardo da Vinci, the Florentine genius who was equally great as a mathematician, naturalist, anatomist, botanist, engineer and artist. In Poland, Copernicus was making the first clear analysis of the movements of the heavenly bodies in an effort to prove that the earth moved around the sun. Tycho Brahe, the Danish astronomer, was improving astronomical instruments and fixing the positions of planets and stars. Johannes Kepler formulated his famous laws of planetary motions.

In 1564, the great scientist, Galileo, was born in

79

Pisa, Italy. At the age of eighteen, he made a discovery which had a tremendous effect upon the subsequent development of clocks.

One day, while in the cathedral at Pisa, he happened to notice a lamp which was suspended from the ceiling. It swung slowly back and forth as a light breeze from the open door stirred it into motion. While he watched, a stronger gust of air caused it to swing more rapidly, so that it described a wider arc. His interest was caught and he began to time the movements of the swinging lamp by his pulse beat. He found that the time for each swing was the same, no matter what the length of the arc happened to be. This led to his famous discovery of the law of the pendulum, in which he presented the theory of *isochronism,* which means equal time.

Galileo's principle was not immediately linked to the making of clocks. More than half a century later, in 1639, he wrote an essay in which he attempted to apply the pendulum to the measurement of time, but he died before the problem was solved.

The principle of isochronism was finally applied to clockmaking by Christian Huygens, the famous Dutch astronomer and mathematician, who discovered the rings of Saturn. About 1665, he devised a clock which used a pendulum to regulate the escapement. Credit for the invention is also claimed for Dr. Robert Hooke.

the English physicist, inventor and mathematician. He was considered by many to have been the greatest mechanic of his time.

Exactly how did the pendulum work? Since each vibration took the same time, it permitted the escapement to release its energy at an absolutely steady rate. Here at last was a simple device that prevented the escapement from speeding up or slowing down.

Other improvements in clock design followed, particularly in the eighteenth century. Escapements were perfected, and various devices were invented to counteract the effects of varying temperatures.

THE WATCH

The first watches were made at the beginning of the sixteenth century by Peter Henlein, the inventor of the mainspring. With the elimination of the hanging weights which furnished the motive power for the old clocks, it became possible to make smaller types which could be placed on tables or anywhere else in the home. Henlein not only made small clocks for domestic use, but he also carried the idea a step further and made clocks small enough to be carried about by people. These small, portable clocks became known as *watches*.

They were very crude, by modern standards, and

81

bore very little resemblance to watches as we know them. They were heavy, bulky and egg-shaped. Because of this, they soon became known as Nuremberg Eggs. Since they were actually miniature clocks, many of them had striking mechanisms and sounded each hour. The entire watch mechanism was enclosed in an egg-shaped case. Part of the case was hinged and could be raised to expose the dial. Like most early clocks, these watches had but one hand to show the hours. The dial was protected by a lattice of pierced metal.

The entire mechanism was made of iron. The wheels of the train and the plates were held in place with tapered pins. Of course, the whole thing was painstakingly constructed by hand. Each part had to be cut, filed and shaped to fit the watch for which it was made.

These early watches kept worse time than the clocks of the period, yet they were in great demand. They were very expensive luxuries; ownership of a watch marked one as a person of wealth and importance, for the common people couldn't possibly afford them. Since only the very wealthy could buy watches in the first place, no expense was spared in their manufacture. Dials and cases became very elaborate and represented the work of the finest jewelers. They were worn very conspicuously, either around the neck on a chain, or fastened to one's belt. When showing off a watch, the owner would proudly exhibit the works, which kept ticking away steadily. People were fascinated by the elaborately engraved mechanism.

Watches were regarded as toys of the rich. They were not seriously considered as timekeepers, for the old foliot escapement was not very dependable. Whenever a watch was moved from a perpendicular position, the foliot would slow down. As a result, a watch could be off by as much as several hours a day. However, this didn't really matter, for time could always be told in a number of other ways. Sundials and clepsydrae were still in common use, and every town had at least one clock in a public place.

As new ideas in timekeeping were developed, they were applied to both clocks and watches. The introduction of the fusee in 1525 made it possible for watches to keep time more accurately. Around 1550 the iron wheels used in watch trains gave way to new types made of brass. At about the same time, the use of screws was introduced, replacing the iron pins which had held the watch movement together. Glass crystals were first put on watches around 1600. Watches with minute-hands appeared around 1673.

The demand for watches grew. Watchmakers learned to make them smaller, and they began to appear in a wide variety of curious forms. It was quite ordinary to

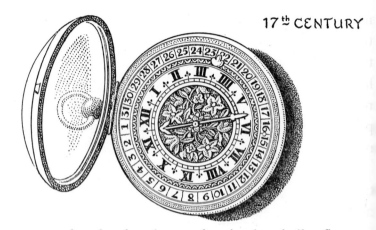

see watches in the shape of animals, shells, flowers, insects, books, crosses—even skulls. Mary, Queen of Scots, gave a skull watch to one of her maids of honor. Watches continued to become more and more elaborate, although they changed very little mechanically. Cases made of gold, silver, agate and rock crystal were available. Some were beautifully decorated with delicate enameling. However, they remained ingenious novelties, with accurate timekeeping a minor factor in their desirability.

Improvements were inevitable, though. By this time the foremost scientists of the age had begun to take an interest in the problems of timekeeping. Christian Huygens, who had first applied the pendulum to clocks invented the *hairspring* in 1674. Dr. Robert Hooke claimed to have invented the same thing in 1660. No

84

matter who deserves credit for the original invention, the hairspring represents a milestone in the science of timekeeping, for it did for watches what the pendulum had done for clocks. It permitted the escapement to release energy in even pulses of equal force. It made possible the production of watches that kept time reliably.

In 1704, Nicholas Facio, a Swiss watchmaker, introduced jewels to watch movements. Most people are not aware of the reason for jewels in watches. In the first place, they really are jewels but, contrary to popular belief, they are worth very little. Wheels in watches were set on tiny axles, or arbors; these had thin ends, known as pivots. In order to keep the wheels in position so that their teeth meshed properly, the pivots were fitted into holes in metal plates. Each watch had an upper and lower plate, which prevented the wheels from moving out of place. As the wheels turned, the pivots gradually wore away the holes in the plates. The holes became enlarged and, as a result, the wheels shifted out of alignment. The teeth no longer meshed as they should, and excessive friction was introduced. The watch would lose time, behave erratically, or stop completely.

Facio conceived the idea of using a very hard substance as bearings for the pivots. He cut tiny, disklike sections of jewels, pierced them with holes of the proper diameter, and set them into the metal plates. The pivots now turned in a hard, highly polished bearing. When properly lubricated, friction was reduced considerably, and pivot wear was practically eliminated.

For many years, real garnets, rubies and sapphires were used. Some watches even had diamonds as jeweled bearings. Modern watchmakers have substituted synthetic stones. These do not have the imperfections of natural jewels and thus guarantee against wear. The number of jewels contained in a watch is not necessarily a measure of its quality, for it is possible to have a fully jeweled watch which is poorly constructed. On the other hand, a good watch can be improved if jewels are applied properly. Some cheap watches manufactured today do not have jewels; these will wear out just as rapidly as did those of the early eighteenth century.

Other problems concerning watchmaking were solved during the eighteenth century. Escapements were perfected, and Swiss watchmakers designed movements that required very little power to make them run. This made it possible to eliminate the fusee and attach the mainspring directly to the wheels. With the thick fusee removed, thin watches could be fashioned very much like the ones in use today.

By this time, watchmaking was in the hands of the manufacturers, who diligently tried to improve their products in order to increase sales. Until the middle of the nineteenth century, watch parts were made by hand. This was a costly process, and watches were expensive as a result. American manufacturers introduced mass-production methods; prices dropped and almost anyone could own a watch.

Watches were no longer playthings of the wealthy. They had become practical timekeepers, essential to everyone.

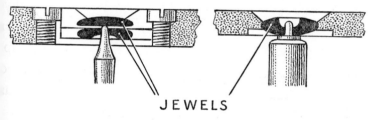

JEWELS

4

TIME AND NAVIGATION

AGES ago, men discovered Polaris, the North Star. No matter how the other heavenly bodies moved in the sky, Polaris remained in the same position. Men learned to find their way by referring to this fixed star. When they took to the sea, they discovered that other stars, too, could serve as their guides.

There is evidence that long before recorded history primitive men not only undertook long sea voyages, but also made maps of the regions in which they lived.

Why did men venture far out on the unknown sea? What prompted them to leave their homes to face perils of which they had no conception? In the beginning, it may have been a search for new sources of food. Later, we know that the motivating force was a desire for conquest, colonization, or trade.

As civilizations expanded, they depended more and more upon the products of other lands. This meant the

88

development of trade on a large scale. About 3000 B.C., Egyptian ships sailed to Spain to trade in bronze and tin. During the same period, they also made regular voyages to a land they called Punt. This is believed to be on the Zambesi River, in what is now Southern Rhodesia. According to the Bible, King Solomon, in partnership with the King of Tyre, outfitted a fleet of ships which sailed to the land of Ophir, which was also presumably in Africa, and may have been the land the Egyptians called Punt.

By 600 B.C., the Mediterranean and the Black Sea were thoroughly explored by the Greeks, the Phoenicians and the Carthaginians. The Egyptian Pharoah Necho II is said to have sponsored a Phoenician fleet which sailed around Africa at this time. Herodotus, the Greek historian, recorded the details of this voyage 150 years later.

The Vikings sailed their dragon-headed ships all over the northern seas. They reached Iceland in 863, and landed in North America 500 years before Columbus came to the New World.

The interesting question is this: how did these ancient navigators find their way? Many of these early voyages, particularly in the Mediterranean, were made from one point to another. The ship left one port and, under the influence of a steady wind, simply kept going until it

89

reached its destination. If the wind died down, the sailors took to the oars. The captain corrected his course by observing the stars at night and the position of the sun during the day. Most trips were made in coastal waters within sight of land, and there was not much risk involved.

Sailing charts drawn before the birth of Christ described landmarks, distances from place to place, and the water's depth in certain areas. Sometimes a weighted plummet, smeared with pitch or tallow, was dropped overboard. Bits of matter from the ocean's bed would stick to it, giving the navigator another clue to his whereabouts.

Still, many long voyages were undertaken in strange waters and ships sailed far from land for many days at a time. There was no friendly shore in sight; the sun and stars were the only guides. If the weather remained overcast for any length of time, ship and crew were lost.

When, early in the eleventh century, the compass was introduced, mariners at last had a means of determining their direction no matter what the weather might be. The first compasses were very crude; later, the compass card was marked off in degrees.

Navigators in ancient days knew the *direction* in which they were going, but they were never really certain *how far* they had gone. The captain of a ship would estimate his position by a system known as *dead reckoning,* a term which is derived from "deduced reckoning." He knew the direction of travel. By glancing over the side at the water moving past, he could estimate his rate of speed with fair accuracy. Much later, speed was determined with a log line. The captain then multiplied the unit of speed by the number of hours that had elapsed since the last reading, and then calculated the distance the ship had traveled.

Stated in modern terms, a ship moving northward at 5 miles per hour for 5 hours would cover 25 miles. The captain then drew a north-south line on his chart, representing 25 miles. The northernmost end of the line would show the ship's position. Or, let us suppose a definite course was being followed, in which the ship had to proceed northward for 25 miles. The captain would estimate the speed of his vessel and then determine how long it would take the ship to cover the distance. He would simply divide the distance by the speed, and find the time: $25 \div 5 = 5$ hours.

The best that could be done in this manner was to find the ship's approximate position. Real accuracy was impossible, for the methods of determining both speed and time were crude. Even if an error had not been made in guessing the speed of the ship, there was no exact unit of time measurement. You will recall that in

91

ancient times an hour was reckoned as ½₂ of the period of daylight. No matter how much this daylight period varied, an hour was always stubbornly calculated as ½₂ of the daylight period. Seasonal changes and differences in latitude made it impossible to arrive at hours of equal length.

When, in the thirteenth century, the concept of equal hours was introduced, mariners had a better basis for reckoning time. Clepsydrae and hourglasses were taken aboard ship, where they marked off the hours more or less regularly. We do not know how efficient they were, but we can assume that the ship's motion affected their accuracy. Of the two, the hourglass was more widely used.

The fifteenth century marked the period of great voyages of exploration. The Turks had taken Constantinople in 1453, and thereafter controlled the ancient sea route to the east. Europeans, in an attempt to break this monopoly, sought another way to reach their eastern markets. The quest for gold, drugs, gems and spices forced them to seek a western route to the Indies.

The explorers of that time were well equipped with courage, but their navigation instruments were pitifully inadequate. They used the compass, hourglass, and astrolabe, a crude device for measuring the altitude of heavenly bodies. This was a disk made of wood or

92

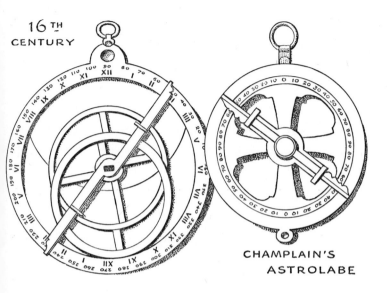

CHAMPLAIN'S
ASTROLABE

metal with the circumference marked off into degrees. The navigator sighted along a pointer arm, then took a reading at the edge of the circle. Navigation was still a matter of dead reckoning. Sailors could not yet tell exactly how far they had gone, and consequently never knew exactly where they were!

Under these circumstances, it seems incredible that the early explorers ever embarked upon their long voyages with such poor equipment. Why did they attempt what we might consider suicidal ventures?

People thought the world was much smaller than it really is. Maps of that time were highly inaccurate; vast areas of land and sea never appeared on these maps, simply because they were unknown. Columbus sailed into an unknown sea with confidence, completely unaware of its size. He never dreamed that two vast continents stood between him and Asia.

By the sixteenth century, it became apparent that accurate navigation would never be possible unless some better way of keeping time at sea could be developed.

The invention of the clock did nothing to improve matters. The early clocks with their hanging weights could not be used on board ship. Clocks could not be used even after the mainspring came into general use, for the motion of the ship made the old foliots behave erratically. The introduction of the pendulum did not solve the problem either, for the pendulum would only work properly if the clock's position was not disturbed. Huygens and Hooke both attempted to construct a pendulum clock which would keep time accurately at sea, but neither succeeded.

Navigation at the time was really a matter of guesswork. The navigator kept his log as accurately as possible. He noted the courses steered and his estimates of the distances covered. He had to make allowances for tides, currents, drifting, poor steering, compass inaccuracies, and his own errors in computation. To this very day, we say that someone is "at sea" when he is befuddled, or doesn't know what is going on around him.

Mapmaking, on the other hand, had become an important art by the sixteenth century. The great cartographers of the age had already published maps of all the known areas of the world. Gerardus Mercator, the famous Flemish geographer, mathematician and cartographer, had invented the form of map projection which still bears his name. Mercator projections are still used by navigators.

However, while navigators could plot their direction with accuracy, they still could not find their exact position. In order to do this, they had to be able to determine both *latitude* and *longitude*.

Examine a global map of the world, and you will find that it is marked off with horizontal and vertical lines. These are used to establish one's north-south and east-west position.

A horizontal line is drawn all around the earth, midway between the North and South Poles; this marks the equator and separates the earth into a Northern and Southern Hemisphere. Latitude is the distance north or south of the equator; it is measured in degrees. The symbol for degree is °. We customarily divide a full circle into 360°. The distance between the two poles on one side of the earth is a half-circle, and is therefore

180°. The equator represents 0° of latitude, and the North and South Poles are each 90° away. The spaces between the poles and the equator are divided evenly by lines called *parallels of latitude;* they are all parallel to the equator. Parallels are spaced 10° apart.

Distances north of the equator are known as *north latitude;* south of the equator, we refer to *south latitude.* The location of any particular place can be given in terms of latitude, which actually indicates its distance from the equator. For example, 1° of latitude is equal to approximately 70 miles. A location described as Lat. 1° N. would be 70 miles north of the equator. A place Lat. 2° S. would be 140 miles south of the equator, and so on. Lat. 90° N. or S. would be at the North or South Poles.

The use of degrees alone would make it impossible to establish latitude closer than 70 miles, so degrees are divided into *minutes,* and minutes into *seconds.* There are 60 minutes (written as 60′) in every degree, and 60 seconds (written as 60″) in every minute. A minute equals about 6,000 feet, or 1 nautical mile. A second is equal to about 100 feet.

Latitude can now be determined with absolute precision. The old navigators found their latitude by "shooting" the sun with an astrolabe, with fairly good results.

Determining longitude was another matter entirely,

96

for this could not be done without the aid of an accurate timepiece. Let us return to our global map and examine the vertical lines that are found on it.

These are known as *meridians of longitude*. They extend from North to South Pole and cross the parallels of latitude at right angles. Each meridian is therefore one half of a cricle. Meridians divide the earth into 360°.

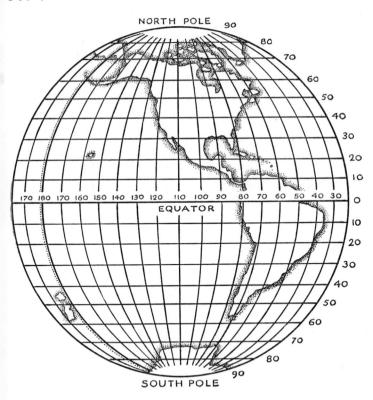

The old mapmakers could not agree as to where 0° ought to be placed, and there was quite a bit of confusion about this point. Finally, in 1884, it was decided by international agreement that 0°, or the *prime meridian,* should be the one that passes through the Royal Observatory at Greenwich, England. The longitude of a place is its distance east or west of the prime meridian. Like latitude, longitude is measured in degrees, minutes, and seconds. Meridians start at 0° at the prime meridian, and go in both directions, up to 180°. The 180th meridian is the same for both east and west longitudes, since it is directly opposite the prime meridian. If one were to draw a line through the prime meridian and the 180th meridian, it would describe a circle that would divide the earth in half.

The earth rotates from west to east once every 24 hours. Since there are 360° of longitude, we can say that it takes the earth 24 hours to turn 360°. To find the number of degrees that the earth turns in 1 hour, simply divide the number of degrees by the number of hours ($360 \div 24 = 15$). This means that there will be a *time difference* of exactly 1 hour for every 15° of longitude. What we are actually saying at this point is that time is equal to distance (1 hour = 15° of longitude).

If you know the time at any given meridian, and you

98

know the time where you are, the difference in time can easily be translated into terms of longitude, or distance. For example, if it is noon at Greenwich (0° longitude), it is 2 hours earlier, or 10:00 A.M. at Long. 30° W. It is 2 hours later, or 2:00 P.M. at Long. 30° E.

Now let us return to the old navigators and their timekeeping problems. It was easy for them to determine their local, or solar time, wherever they might be. Noon could always be fixed with the aid of the astrolabe and noting that moment when the sun was at its zenith, or highest point. Their real problem was the lack of an instrument that would show them the time at the meridian they were using as a point of reference. Existing timekeepers were so inaccurate that when navigators reached what they thought was the end of a long voyage they sometimes found themselves hundreds of miles off course.

The governments of Europe were well aware of the need for improving methods of navigation. Most of them offered rewards for solutions to the problem, but no one came forward with an acceptable plan.

By the eighteenth century, the situation had become desperate. In 1713 the British government appointed a Board of Longitude, whose purpose was to investigate the problem of finding longitude at sea. The leading scientists of the day were consulted, but none had ready

99

answers. Sir Isaac Newton, who was then president of the Royal Society, described several possible methods by which longitude could be determined, but in the same breath conceded that they were not practical for use at sea. He then suggested that a watch be tried, "But by reason of the Motion of a Ship, the Variation of Heat and Cold, Wet and Dry, and the Difference in Gravity in different latitudes, such a Watch hath not yet been made."

Of course, Newton was right. No such watch had yet been made. Early eighteenth-century watches could not keep exact time on land, so they could hardly be expected to meet the rigid requirements imposed by the sea.

Finally, the Board of Longitude convinced the government that a large reward should be offered for "any generally practicable and useful method of finding longitude at sea." Accordingly, a reward of from £10,000 to £20,000 was offered. An inventor's device would be tested at sea; the prize money would be awarded according to the amount of error found at the end of a voyage lasting six weeks. If the error amounted to thirty miles or less, he would be entitled to the full reward of £20,000. The sum was reduced to £10,000 for an error of sixty miles.

This was the largest sum of money that had ever

been offered for this purpose. The reward was sought by clockmakers and scientists all over Europe. You will recall that both Christian Huygens and Dr. Robert Hooke experimented with pendulum clocks that would keep time on board ship, but neither one succeeded.

For seventeen years the problem remained unsolved. Then, in 1729, a young man arrived in London determined to try for the reward. His name was John Harrison, and he was the son of a carpenter of Foulby, Yorkshire. He had been trained as a carpenter, but his real interest lay in clocks. As a boy he had been fascinated by mechanisms of all kinds. Completely self-taught, and without any formal training, he had learned to repair and build clocks. At the age of twenty-two, he had constructed an 8-day clock entirely of wood.

Harrison went directly to the Board of Longitude, bringing the plans for a clock he had designed. He asked for financial assistance, so that he might devote his time to working on the construction of the clock. The Board not only refused to advance him any money, but treated the whole matter in a very discouraging fashion.

Edmund Halley, the famous astronomer who predicted the return of the comet which has been named after him, was then Astronomer Royal at the Greenwich Observatory. He became interested in Harrison and introduced him to George Graham, who was con-

101

sidered the finest watchmaker of that time. Graham was a man of many accomplishments. In addition to having contributed important inventions to the science of watchmaking, he was an astronomer and a Fellow of the Royal Society. After he examined Harrison's plans, he urged the young man to develop them. Furthermore, he advanced him the money he needed without security of any kind.

Free from financial pressure, Harrison went to work on his chronometer. Six years later, in 1735, it was completed. He had created a timekeeper which incorporated many original ideas of great ingenuity. In its design, he had taken special precautions against excessive friction and errors due to temperature and motion. It was a large machine, weighing more than 70 pounds.

The following year, Harrison submitted the chronometer to the Board of Longitude. It was placed on board H.M.S. *Centurion* for testing on a voyage to Lisbon. Harrison went along on the trial journey. The captain of the ship navigated by the customary method of dead reckoning, while Harrison referred to the chronometer exclusively. After a few days, Harrison's observations placed the ship about seventy miles west of the position arrived at by the captain, and they turned out to be correct.

102

The chronometer had performed astonishingly well and, on the strength of this, the Board advanced him a little money for the construction of an improved version. Number Two took two years to build, and turned out to be an improvement over the first one. Unfortunately, it was never tested at sea. Britain was engaged in a war with Spain at the time, and the Admiralty did not want to risk losing what was unquestionably the world's best timekeeper.

At any rate, Harrison's second chronometer was set aside, and he began the construction of a third one. This was a mechanical masterpiece, quite different in design from the first two. It was begun in 1740 and finished in 1757—seventeen years later. He now announced that he was ready to try for the reward of £20,000. However, before making the test, he decided to construct another chronometer, to be used as a check on the accuracy of Number Three.

Once again Harrison went to work, this time to create a timepiece that was far different from any he had yet built. Where the others had been heavy machines, Number Four was less than 6 inches in diameter—actually a large watch. It was constructed with almost incredible skill and precision, and contained many new design features. Tests proved that it kept time just as well as the third chronometer. Since it was smaller,

103

lighter and more portable, Harrison decided to submit this one for the prize money. The third chronometer, for which Number Four had been constructed as an auxiliary, was put aside. This, after laboring over it for seventeen years!

In 1761 Harrison and his timepiece boarded H.M.S. *Deptford* and set sail for Jamaica. Once again, the captain navigated by dead reckoning, while Harrison made his own observations according to his chronometer. As they approached the island of Madeira, it became evident that either Harrison or the captain had made an error, for there was a difference of 1½ ° in their calculations of longitude. Since they had been at sea only nine days, this was a matter of great concern; it meant that one of them had miscalculated the ship's position by about 100 miles.

The captain insisted that Harrison was wrong. He was certain that if they relied on the chronometer they would miss Madeira altogether. But Harrison had faith in his instrument. The ship kept to his course, and Madeira was sighted the following day, exactly where Harrison's calculations had placed it.

The voyage to Jamaica took nine weeks. At the end of that time Harrison's chronometer was off by only 5 seconds, which meant an error of longitude of less than a mile! This was truly astonishing accuracy. Harrison

104

HARRISON'S
WORLD - FAMOUS
"NUMBER FOUR"

felt certain that he had earned the reward at long last.

However, back in London, the Board of Longitude refused to give him the £20,000 to which he felt he was entitled. They claimed that the remarkable performance of his chronometer was purely accidental. They very reluctantly gave him £2,500, and insisted on another series of tests before they would part with another penny. They evidently felt that no timepiece could possibly be as accurate as Harrison's had proved itself to be.

The chronometer was tested a second time on a five-month voyage to Barbados. Again it proved its superlative timekeeping ability, for at the end of that time it had lost a grand total of 15 seconds.

Now there seemed to be no doubt about the chronometer's accuracy and practicability. Harrison again applied for the reward, and once more the Board refused to grant it. This time they demanded that he write a book explaining the mechanism, so that other watchmakers might understand it. Then they would pay him an additional sum of £7,500. Harrison complied with this request, and the Board paid him the money.

By this time Harrison had received £10,000, half the money to which he was entitled. The Board of Longitude agreed to give him the other half if he would construct two more chronometers, equal in accuracy to Number Four.

This seemed like an impossible assignment, for he was now past seventy years of age, and his sight was not equal to the task. However, he finally managed to make another watch, a copy of his fourth chronometer, but he could do no more.

Still the Board refused to pay him the final installment of £10,000, and it seemed as though he would never get it. Finally his plight came to the attention of King George III, who used his influence to bring the affair to a conclusion. Harrison presented a petition to Parliament, where the matter was taken up. Indignant questions were asked, and Harrison's shabby treatment was given publicity. Such a storm of protest was stirred up that the Board had to pay him the remaining £10,000.

Harrison lived three years after receiving the final portion of the reward; he died in 1776 at the age of eighty-two. He had spent fifty years on his project and managed to accomplish what the best scientists of the century had failed to do.

His remarkable instruments have influenced the construction of marine chronometers since that time. They have been preserved by the British government and still keep excellent time.

Captain Cook, the famous English explorer, used a copy of Harrison's chronometer on his second and third Antarctic voyages. There is no doubt that this made it possible for him to prepare the precise maps and charts for which he was so well known. England's expanding colonial empire called for a large number of ships, and accurate navigation was essential. Harrison's invention transformed navigation from guesswork to an exact science.

5

TIME AND SCIENCE

MANY branches of modern science have reached their present state of development only because it is possible to make precise measurements of time intervals. Definitions of scientific phenomena are often expressed in terms of time.

Electricity is thought to be the movement of electrons along a conductor. The strength of electric currents is measured in *amperes*. The amount of electricity which is provided by a current of one ampere flowing *for one second* is called a *coulomb*. This definition would be meaningless if we were to leave out the phrase, "for one second."

Other basic aspects of electricity are related to time. Certain types of electrical generators produce alternating current, which changes its direction of flow periodically. The current first flows along a wire in one direction (from positive to negative), and then reverses itself and flows in the other direction (from negative to positive). Two reversals of current direction are known as a *cycle*. The number of current changes is expressed in *cycles per second;* this is also called the frequency of the current.

Most homes in the United States are wired for 60-cycle current. Every time you turn on a lamp or other electrical appliance, the current which flows through it reverses itself 120 times each second. There remain a few areas in the country where electric current is still supplied at a frequency of 25 or 50 cycles, but 60-cycle current is practically standard throughout the country.

The vast field of electronics is also concerned with time. Broadcasting stations send out radio waves which do not depend upon wires but travel through the air. Each station has been assigned a broadcasting frequency, from which it may not vary. The dial of a typical radio receiver is marked with numerals ranging from about 550 to 1600; these represent *kilocycles* (abbreviated as *kc*). One kilocycle is equal to 1,000 cycles. When you tune in a station at 550 kc, your set is receiving a radio wave that has been generated at the rate of 550 kc, or 550,000 cycles *per second*. At the other end of the dial, a station would be broadcasting a 1,600,000-cycle (1600 kc) wave.

109

Radio waves can be generated from about 20,000 to several *billion* cycles per second. Compare this with the 60-cycle current found in your home.

Radio stations are also concerned with time in another way. Programs and station announcements are broadcast according to a very rigid time schedule. Should a program run even slightly past its allotted time, it is cut off the air. The next scheduled program starts "on the nose," which means *exactly on time*.

We are accustomed to measuring time in short intervals. Stop watches can time fractions of a second. Your watch indicates seconds, minutes, and hours. Calendars show the passing of days, weeks, months, and years. Historical studies may span hundreds, sometimes thousands of years.

Geologists, who make a study of the history of the earth, are interested in much longer time intervals. For example, they have determined that the Ice Age in New England ended about 25,000 years ago. At one time, this area was covered by an immense glacier. Streams formed by the melting ice caught up particles of sediment and carried them into nearby lakes. This sediment was deposited on the lake floors. During the warmer spring and summer months, the ice melted more rapidly; the streams became larger and faster, and picked up more and heavier particles. During fall and winter, the

110

flow of water in the streams slowed down; smaller particles were carried to the lakes.

As a result of this stream action, deposits of clay laid down in a lake often show alternating layers of fine and coarse particles. The coarse matter was carried down during the spring and summer; the finer clays settled during the winter. These layers are called *varves;* a pair of varves represents one year. Scientists have examined the land in New England that once was covered by the glacier and counted varves in ancient glacial lakes. Clays containing 25,000 double layers have been found, indicating that the glacier retreated 25,000 years ago.

Another method of estimating geological time involves studying the rate at which rivers deposit sediment on the ocean floor. It has been determined that it takes from 5,000 to 10,000 years for one foot of sedimentary material to be formed. This means that a rock deposit 100 feet thick is between 500,000 and 1,000,000 years old. Since there is such a wide variation in the rate of deposition, this method is not too accurate. However, it can be used to tell the approximate age of certain sedimentary rocks.

How old is the earth? In the early days of science, the earth's age was a matter of pure guesswork, for no one had found a reliable method of obtaining the answer.

Modern science has furnished us with a clue to this puzzle. It has been found that certain radioactive substances like uranium and thorium give off tiny particles. This causes them to disintegrate, or decay, and eventually turn to lead. This decay takes place at a definite, known rate. The rate of decay is found by determining the *half-life* of each substance, which is the time it takes for half the atoms to decay. Each radioactive material has a particular half-life, which does not change. For example, let us assume that the half-life of a certain substance is 10 years. This means that at the end of 10 years, exactly half the atoms of which it is composed will have disintegrated. If we start with 1 gram of this substance, 10 years later there will be ½ gram left. In another 10 years, or 2 half-lives later, we will have only half of this amount, or ¼ gram. This goes on indefinitely, exactly half of the remainder decaying during each subsequent half-life.

Scientists are thus furnished with a very accurate atomic clock. Certain types of rocks contain traces of radioactive elements. Samples of rock are analyzed, and the proportion of radioactive material to lead is determined. Since atomic decay produces lead, the more lead a rock contains, the older it is.

Uranium-238 has a half-life of 4,500,000,000 years. Geologists have discovered rocks containing mostly lead, and a very small proportion of uranium. This indicates that these rocks were formed a very long time ago. By calculation, some have been found to be more than two billion years old! On the basis of these and other findings, the earth's age has been estimated at about three billion years.

Archaeologists, who study the lives and cultures of ancient people, are very much interested in methods of establishing the age of objects. Many old cities have been excavated, after having been buried for thousands of years. Objects found at these sites are removed and carefully studied for clues to the past. Very often nothing is found but ruins, which sometimes indicate that a city was destroyed by fire, or as a result of war. Despite the condition in which objects are found, it is possible to determine their age if they are vegetable or animal in origin.

This is done by making use of another type of atomic clock. All living things contain carbon-14, a radioactive form of carbon. When they die, this carbon-14 begins to disintegrate. Since the half-life, or rate of decay of carbon-14 is known, the age of a specimen can be determined with accuracy. The radioactive particles given off by such things as bits of bone from a refuse heap can be measured for their radioactivity, dating the site at which they are found. A specimen of wood from

113

the beam of a house can be analyzed to find the age of the structure.

Astronomy is so closely allied with time that we cannot speak of one subject without involving the other. As we know, our entire concept of time is based on the actual motions of the earth and the apparent motions of other heavenly bodies.

Astronomers use *time* as a basis for measuring *distance*. To understand this, we must make an attempt to visualize the immensities of space, and the simply incredible distances that are involved.

Let us begin with the earth, which has a circumference of approximately 25,000 miles. The nearest heavenly body is the moon, which is about 238,000 miles away. The distance from the earth to the moon is more than 95 times the distance around the earth. If you could hop into a space ship and take off for the moon, you would reach it in about 100 days—provided you moved at a speed of about 1,000 miles per hour. A trip to the moon is within the realm of possibility, for, astronomically speaking, the moon is right next door.

The sun, which is the center of our solar system, is very much farther away—93,000,000 miles. In case you are interested in traveling this distance, you ought to know that at 1,000 miles per hour, it would take 93,000 hours, or 3,875 days, or more than 10½ years!

114

Yet, considering the vast distances between the earth and the stars, the sun is very close indeed. The nearest star, Proxima Centauri, is about 250,000 times as far away as the sun. This is a distance of about 25,500,000,-000,000 miles. The star Arcturus is about 188,000,-000,000,000 miles away from the earth.

Astronomers do not use miles when calculating distances in space; they are much too small as measuring units. Instead, they use a unit known as a *light-year,* which is the distance that a ray of light travels in one year. Since the speed of light is 186,000 miles *per second,* one light-year is equal to about 6,000,000,000,000 miles. Proxima Centauri is therefore 4⅓ light-years away, and Arcturus is *32* light-years away. This means that the ray of light which now reaches us from Arcturus started on its way *32* years ago, and has taken all that time to reach us. Powerful, modern telescopes can bring us images from a distance of more than a billion light-years. Thus, from an astronomical point of view, time equals distance.

Let us come back to earth again, and find other instances of time used as a measure of distance. A stranger, asking directions, might be told that the place he seeks is "about 5 minutes' walk." In these days of high-speed transportation, people often refer to distances by using time units. An air traveler may know that Chicago is about 3 hours from New York by plane, yet he may not know how far apart the two cities are in miles. Of course, these standards change with the times. As air speeds increase, time of travel is reduced.

We have seen how time enters into the study of electronics, geology, archaeology and astronomy. It is possible to find many other examples to show how time and science are related. This relationship is so close that we might say science depends upon time.

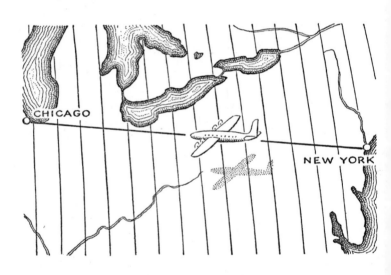

MODERN TIMEKEEPING

TIME reckoned by the position of the sun is known as *solar time, sun time,* or *local time.* Solar noon is that time of day when the sun reaches its zenith, or highest point in the sky. Imagine a line in the sky, running from north to south. This is the *observer's meridian.* It is noon at the exact moment the sun crosses this meridian. Noon can also be determined roughly by observing the shadow of a vertical stick held against a flat, horizontal surface; when the shadow is shortest, it is noon.

As the earth rotates from west to east, the sun seems to move from east to west. We call this the *apparent* motion of the sun, for we know that the sun does not really move. Because of the rotation of the earth and the sun's apparent motion, it is always noon somewhere on earth.

We know that a time difference of 1 hour exists for every 15° of longitude. This can be broken down still

117

further: 1° of longitude represents a time difference of 4 minutes. If it is noon where you are, it is 11:56 A.M. (4 minutes earlier), 1° longitude west of you, and it is 12:04 P.M. (4 minutes later), 1° east of you. In other words, if there is a difference in longitude between two places, there must be a corresponding difference in local time. This seems obvious, since local time is reckoned according to the position of the sun, and the sun's position differs with respect to each place.

Now let us suppose that each village and city used local time. Each would have its own timekeeping system. No two places would have the same time, unless they were located on the same meridian of longitude. Time differences of from several seconds to several minutes would exist among cities in the same general area.

This was the actual state of affairs in the United States and other countries for many years. Each city kept time its own way, depending upon its own particular local time.

Variations in local time did not matter very much in the old days, for life went on at a leisurely pace, and most people's activities revolved around their home towns. However, as speedier methods of communication and transportation developed, activities took on a countrywide and, of course, international scope. The situation became very confusing and kept getting worse.

118

As railroads extended their lines across the country, they found themselves in trouble. They would run trains according to their schedules, but at each stop they would find a different system of timekeeping in use. As each railroad kept its own time, which was not necessarily the same as that of other railroads, things became even more complicated.

This confusing situation existed until 1883, when the American railroads adopted a system of *standard time*. The following year, at an international conference held in Washington, D.C., standard time was adopted on a world-wide basis; this is the time we now use.

At that time Greenwich was established as the prime meridian, with a longitude of 0°. The time at Green-

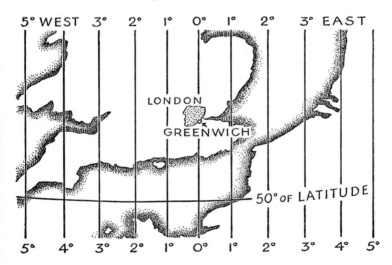

wich is accepted as a standard, from which time all over the world is reckoned.

Every 15th meridian of longitude east and west of Greenwich is designated as a *time meridian,* which serves as the center of a *time belt,* or zone, 15° wide. The earth is divided into twenty-four time belts. Since the time meridians are 15° apart, there is a difference of 1 hour's time between them. Under standard time, the time at each meridian is that kept *for the entire belt.*

The United States has four time belts:

Time Belt	Longitude of Time Meridian
Eastern	75° West
Central	90° West
Mountain	105° West
Pacific	120° West

The time belt boundaries are not perfectly straight lines, for this would be impractical. They would cut across state and city lines and create timekeeping problems. Wherever it has been possible to do so, these boundaries have been altered to make timekeeping more convenient in certain areas. As a result, the time meridians are not always found in the exact center of each belt, but each belt averages 15° in width.

120

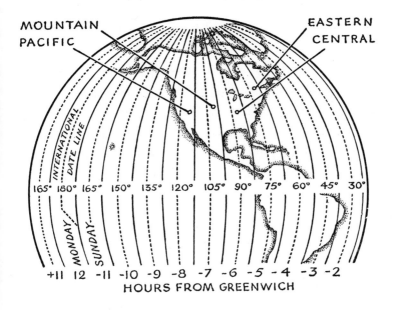

MOUNTAIN   EASTERN
PACIFIC   CENTRAL

165° 180° 165° 150° 135° 120° 105° 90° 75° 60° 45° 30°

+11 12 -11 -10 -9 -8 -7 -6 -5 -4 -3 -2
HOURS FROM GREENWICH

Since there is a time difference of 1 hour between zones, finding out the time in any part of the country is a simple matter. Just subtract one hour for every zone west of you, and add an hour for every zone to the east. If it is noon in New York City (Eastern belt), then it is 11:00 A.M. in Kansas City (Central belt), 10:00 A.M. in Salt Lake City (Mountain belt), and 9:00 A.M. in San Francisco (Pacific belt).

During the late spring and summer months, many places in the United States use *daylight-saving* time. Clocks are advanced one hour ahead of standard time, so that people can take advantage of an additional hour

121

of daylight. This results in a substantial economy, as it cuts out one hour during which electricity would otherwise be used for lighting homes and factories. At the end of the period of daylight-saving, clocks are turned back to standard time.

The U.S. Naval Observatory in Washington, D.C., sets the timekeeping standards for the United States. By means of a device known as a photographic zenith tube, stars are photographed at the exact moment they cross the meridian, an imaginary north-south line in the sky. At the same instant, a signal is produced which is compared with the time as shown on a very accurate master clock. Since the time of each star's transit (the interval between two successive passages through the meridian) is known, any error found in the master clock can be corrected at once. Time signals from the observatory are broadcast by Station NSS, the Naval Radio Station at Annapolis.

The observatory also supplies the Bureau of Standards with the correct time. The Bureau has its own supremely accurate clocks and broadcasts the time from its radio station, WWV. These time signals are broadcast continuously on 5 different frequencies, and are accurate to within 2 parts in 100 million! You can pick up these signals with an ordinary short-wave receiver.

The signals from the Bureau of Standards serve as ex-

122

tremely accurate yardsticks not only for measuring time, but also for the exact determination of frequency. Radio stations must keep their transmitters tuned to their assigned frequencies, and are permitted variations of about .002 per cent. Radio engineers check their broadcasting frequencies with a frequency meter, a very accurate instrument. However, in order to be certain they are calibrated properly, meters are checked against signals from WWV, which vary less than .000002 per cent.

Power companies use WWV signals to adjust their generators so that they produce current of the correct frequency. Among other things, this makes it possible for us to use electric clocks, which operate on 60-cycle current. An electric clock uses a synchronous motor, the speed of which is determined by the frequency of the current with which it is supplied. If the current frequency varies, the motor speed will vary in the same proportion. This means that an electric clock will slow up if the current frequency falls below 60 cycles, and it will run faster if the frequency is higher than 60 cycles. Since the frequency of the electric current supplied to our homes is closely controlled, electric clocks are very accurate.

The modern watch is a remarkable instrument. It contains about 120 parts, which are fitted together to make a mechanism of almost incredible precision.

Despite all the improvements which have been made

123

in watches, they still have the same basic features as those found in the Nuremberg Eggs of 450 years ago. Every watch has a source of power, a means of reducing this power, and a regulating device. The power source is the mainspring; the mainspring's force is reduced and transmitted to the hands by means of a train of wheels; the escapement regulates the speed at which the force is released, and can be adjusted to make the watch run faster or slower.

If you look into the back of a watch, you will see a little wheel swinging back and forth as the watch ticks. This is the *balance wheel,* which might be considered the heart of the watch. Each movement of the balance wheel permits a tiny pulse of energy to be released.

In most watches, the balance wheel swings back and forth, or vibrates, 5 times per second, 300 times per minute, 18,000 times per hour, 432,000 times per day—and 157,680,000 times per year!

The balance wheel in the average wrist watch is about $3/8''$ in diameter; at each vibration its rim will move $3/4''$. It performs an astonishing amount of work:

In 1 second, the balance wheel moves 3.5 inches.

In 1 minute, it moves 210 inches, or 17.5 feet.

In 1 hour, it moves 12,600 inches, or 1,050 feet.

In 1 day, it moves 25,200 feet, or about 4¾ miles.

In 1 year, it moves 1,742 miles.

124

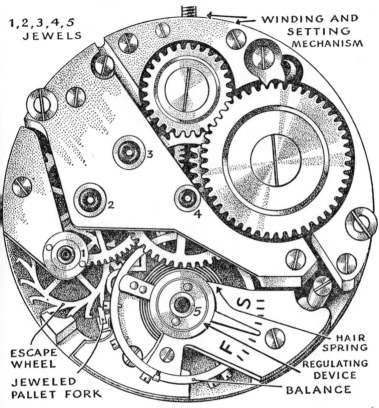

In one year, the balance wheel in your wrist watch actually moves a greater distance than the average person walks in the same length of time!

Early watches were not very accurate, for they could not run equally well in different positions. In most cases, shifting the watch from a perpendicular position would cause it to slow down. Modern escapement design has

125

eliminated errors due to position. This is particularly important in wrist watches, which are constantly being moved on the wearer's wrist.

Temperature changes also affected these early watches. Metal expands when it is heated and shrinks as it cools. If the temperature went up, the balance wheel would expand and become larger in diameter. This very slight difference in size made it vibrate at a slower rate, so that the watch lost time. When subjected to cold, the balance wheel would shrink and become slightly smaller, so that it ran faster. These errors have been eliminated in modern watches. Balance wheels are now made of special alloys which are not sensitive to temperature changes.

At first, all watches were made entirely by hand. Each part was fabricated by the watchmaker and carefully fitted into the movement. Later, this work was given out to private contractors, who would specialize in making certain watch parts. These were returned to the factory, where the watches were assembled. However, each part still had to be fitted to the movement; this had to be done by a skilled watchmaker, who would file, shape and polish it wherever necessary.

Today, the situation is quite different. Watch parts are mass-produced by precision machines. They are made to such exact tolerances that any part will fit any

126

watch of the same type. By tolerance we mean the allowable differences in size that may be found among parts of the same kind. Since watch parts are so small, such differences are really minute. This simplifies watch repairing, too. Whereas in the old days a watchmaker actually had to make each replacement part, today he simply orders an exact duplicate, made by the factory that produced the watch.

We are all familiar with electric clocks; most of us have them in our homes. They never have to be wound and will keep time with great accuracy, provided the flow of current is not interrupted. In 1952, an electric watch was introduced. For the first time since 1500, when Peter Henlein invented the mainspring, a new power source was used in a watch. This is a tiny battery, or energy capsule, about the size of an aspirin tablet. The capsule runs an equally tiny motor, which takes the place of the mainspring. The watch will run for at least a year before the battery has to be replaced.

Another instrument which records elapsed time accurately is the *chronograph*. Some models can time intervals from ⅕ of a second to 12 hours. *Calendar* watches may show days of the week, months, and phases of the moon—in addition to keeping regular time. *Waterproof* watches have special cases, designed to keep the movement dry even if the watch is held under water.

127

These usually have backs which screw into place, exerting pressure against gaskets made of rubber or plastic. The crystals are made of clear plastic and are fitted into the case to form a watertight seal. At one time, the market was flooded with watches which were supposed to be waterproof, but they turned out not to be when put to the test. Since then, governmental standards have been set up to which watchmakers must adhere. Each watch must be marked so that the buyer knows exactly what he is getting. Some watches are marked water-resistant, in which case the manufacturer does not guarantee that they will not be affected by water.

The latest thoughts about watch design are centered around an atomic-powered watch. It has been found that certain substances produce an electric current when exposed to radiation. Scientists are seriously considering the possibility of using miniature power plants of this type inside watches. Such a watch would not necessarily have a conventional movement. A tiny amount of radioactive material would cause some substance to produce electricity. This could conceivably be used to produce vibrations in another material. For example, an electrical charge applied to quartz will cause it to vibrate. These vibrations might very well serve as a means of regulating the watch.

Or, it might be possible to produce a vibrating frequency from which one pulse could be tapped off every second. This could be used to indicate time directly, without even using hands. The pulses could control a flow of electrons which might strike a dial and produce a visible time signal, in the same manner that an electronic flow produces a picture on a television screen.

Of course, many problems have to be solved before the nuclear watch is actually produced. Its construction is scientifically possible, and it is merely a question of time before someone designs a working model. Imagine a watch that never needs cleaning or adjustment and will keep accurate time for about 200 years or so!

How accurate are our watches today? The average good watch will keep time to within a few seconds a day. This is a far cry from the old days, when a man would glance at his watch and then head for the nearest sundial in order to check on its accuracy. We have come a long way from the purely ornamental watch.

VERTICAL SUNDIAL

INDEX

About the Author

Harry Zarchy has lived in and around New York all his life. For many years he has taught fine arts, ceramics, and crafts in New York City high schools and to adult groups as well.

He is a man with an amazing number of interests. Fishing, model trains, and music are some of them. He has played the violin, the banjo, guitar, cello, trumpet, and is now a free-lance bass player. Working once as a watchmaker, he developed a curiosity about old time pieces which led to the writing of this book. He has also worked as a house painter, carpenter, cabinetmaker, counter man in a restaurant, and a waiter.

His house is full of electronic gadgets, such as an intercom system and an amateur radio station. He is a licensed "ham" operator and likes to relax by chatting with other amateurs.

Mr. Zarchy is the author of many excellent books for young people. Now he makes his home on Long Island with his wife and two children.